经典的回声·ECHO OF CLASSICS

孙子兵法
Sunzi: The Art of War
孙膑兵法
Sun Bin: The Art of War

吴如嵩　吴显林　**校释**

林戊荪　**英译**

Edited and translated into modern Chinese by
Wu Rusong and Wu Xianlin

Translated into English by
Lin Wusun

外文出版社
FOREIGN LANGUAGES PRESS

图书在版编目（CIP）数据

孙子兵法·孙膑兵法/吴如嵩，吴显林校释；林戊荪译.
—北京：外文出版社，2001．8
(经典的回声)
ISBN 7-119-02886-3

I. 孙…　II. ①吴… ② 吴… ③林…　III. 英语—对照读物，兵法—汉、英
IV. H319.4:E

中国版本图书馆 CIP 数据核字（2001）第 042721 号

外文出版社网址：
http://www.flp.com.cn
外文出版社电子信箱：
info@flp.com.cn
sales@flp.com.cn

经典的回声（汉英对照）

孙子兵法　孙膑兵法

校　　释	吴如嵩　吴显林
译　　者	林戊荪
责任编辑	胡开敏
封面设计	席恒青
印刷监制	蒋育勤
出版发行	外文出版社
社　　址	北京市百万庄大街 24 号　　　　邮政编码　100037
电　　话	（010）68320579（总编室）
	（010）68329514 / 68327211（推广发行部）
印　　刷	三河市汇鑫印务有限公司
经　　销	新华书店 / 外文书店
开　　本	大 32 开　　　　　　　　字　　数　180 千字
印　　张	11.25
版　　次	2005 年 7 月第 1 版第 4 次印刷
装　　别	平装
书　　号	ISBN 7-119-02886-3 / I　691（外）
定　　价	14.00 元

出 版 前 言

　　本社专事外文图书的编辑出版,几十年来用英文翻译出版了大量的中国文学作品和文化典籍,上自先秦,下迄现当代,力求全面而准确地反映中国文学及中国文化的基本面貌和灿烂成就。这些英译图书均取自相关领域著名的、权威的作品,英译则出自国内外译界名家。每本图书的编选、翻译过程均极其审慎严肃,精雕细琢,中文作品及相应的英译版本均堪称经典。

　　我们意识到,这些英译精品,不单有对外译介的意义,而且对国内英文学习者、爱好者及英译工作者,也是极有价值的读本。为此,我们对这些英译精品做了认真的遴选,编排成汉英对照的形式,陆续推出,以飨读者。

外文出版社

Publisher's Note

Foreign Languages Press is dedicated to the editing, translating and publishing of books in foreign languages. Over the past several decades it has published, in English, a great number of China's classics and records as well as literary works from the Qin down to modern times, in the aim to fully display the best part of the Chinese culture and its achievements. These books in the original are famous and authoritative in their respective fields, and their English translations are masterworks produced by notable translators both at home and abroad. Each book is carefully compiled and translated with minute precision. Consequently, the English versions as well as their Chinese originals may both be rated as classics.

It is generally considered that these English translations are not only significant for introducing China to the outside world but also useful reading materials for domestic English learners and translators. For this reason, we have carefully selected some of these books, and will publish them successively in Chinese-English bilingual form.

Foreign Languages Press

目　　录
CONTENTS

孙子兵法

SUNZI: THE ART OF WAR

孙膑兵法

SUN BIN: THE ART OF WAR

附录:佚书辑录

APPENDIX: COLLECTION OF SCATTERED TEXTS

孙子兵法

Sunzi: The Art of War

计 篇

【原文】

孙子曰：兵者，国之大事，死生之地，存亡之道，不可不察也。

故经之以五事，校之以计而索其情：一曰道，二曰天，三曰地，四曰将，五曰法。

道者，令民与上同意也。故可以与之死，可以与之生，而不畏危。

【今译】

孙子说：战争，是国家的大事，是军队生死的所在，国家存亡的途径，不能不认真考察。

所以，要从五个方面进行分析，比较敌我双方的各种条件，以探索战争的情势：一是道，二是天，三是地，四是将，五是法。

所谓"道"，就是使民众与君主的意愿一致。这样，他们就可以为君主死，为君主生，而不畏惧危险。

2

Making Assessments

Sunzi said:

War is a question of vital importance to the state, a matter of life and death, the road to survival or ruin. Hence, it is a subject which calls for careful study.

To assess the outcome of a war, we need to examine the belligerent parties and compare them in terms of the following five fundamental factors:

The first is the way (*dao* 道); the second, heaven (*tian* 天); the third, earth (*di* 地); the fourth, command (*jiang* 将); and the fifth, rules and regulations (*fa* 法).

By "the way", I mean moral influence, or that which causes the people to think in line with their sovereign so that they will follow him through every vicissitude, whether to live or to die, without fear of mortal peril.

【原文】

天者,阴阳、寒暑、时制也。

地者,远近、险易、广狭、死生也。

将者,智、信、仁、勇、严也。

法者,曲制、官道、主用也。

凡此五者,将莫不闻,知之者胜,不知者不胜。

【今译】

所谓"天",是指昼夜阴晴、寒冬酷暑、春夏秋冬的变化更替。

所谓"地",是指远途近路、险阻平地、地域宽窄、死地生地。

所谓"将",是指将帅的智谋、诚信、仁慈、勇敢、严明。

所谓"法",是指军队的组织编制、将吏的管理、军需的掌管。

凡属这五个方面的情况,将帅都不能不知道。了解这些情况的就能胜利,不了解这些情况的就不能胜利。

By "heaven", I mean the effects of night and day, of good and bad weather, of winter's cold and summer's heat; in short, the conduct of military operations in accordance with the changes of natural forces.

By "earth", I mean distance, whether it is great or small; the terrain, whether it is treacherous or secure; the land, whether it is open or constricted; and the place, whether it portends life or death.

By "command", I mean the wisdom, trustworthiness, benevolence, courage and firmness of the commander.

By "rules and regulations", I mean the principles guiding the organization of army units, the appointment and administration of officers and the management of military supplies and expenditures.

There is no general who has not heard of these five factors. Yet it is he who masters them that wins and he who does not that los-

5

【原文】

故校之以计而索其情，曰：主孰有道？将孰有能？天地孰得？法令孰行？兵众孰强？士卒孰练？赏罚孰明？吾以此知胜负矣。

将听吾计，用之必胜，留之；将不听吾计，用之必败，去之。

计利以听，乃为之势，以佐其外。势者，因利而制权也。

【今译】

所以，要通过对双方情况的比较来探索战争的情势。就是说：哪一方君主更贤明？哪一方将帅更有才能？哪一方天时地理有利？哪一方法令能贯彻执行？哪一方武器装备精良？哪一方兵卒训练有素？哪一方赏罚严明？我根据这些就可以判断谁胜谁负了。

如果听从我的计谋，作战一定胜利，我就留下；如果不听从我的计谋，作战一定失败，我就离去。

分析利害得失的意见已被采纳，然后就要造成有利的态势，作为外在的辅助条件。所谓有利的态势，就是根据对自己有利的情况，掌握作战主动权。

es. Therefore, when assessing the outcome of a war, compare the two sides in terms of the above factors and appraise the situation accordingly.

Find out which sovereign possesses more moral influence, which general is more capable, which side has the advantages of heaven and earth, which army is better disciplined, whose troops are better armed and trained, which command is more impartial in meting out rewards and punishments, and I will be able to forecast which side will be victorious.

The general who employs my assessment methods is bound to win; I shall therefore stay with him. The general who does not heed my words will certainly lose; I shall leave him.

Having paid heed to my assessment of the relative advantages and disadvantages, the general must create a favorable strategic situation which will help bring the victory to fruition. By this I mean being flexible and making the most of the advantages to gain the initiative in war.

【原文】

兵者,诡道也。故能而示之不能,用而示之不用,近而示之远,远而示之近;利而诱之,乱而取之,实而备之,强而避之,怒而挠之,卑而骄之,佚而劳之,亲而离之。攻其无备,出其不意。此兵家之胜,不可先传也。

夫未战而庙算胜者,得算多也,未战而庙

【今译】

用兵应以诡诈为原则。所以,能打而装作不能打,要打而装作不要打,向近处而装作向远处,向远处而装作向近处贪利,就引诱它;敌人混乱,就攻取它;敌人力量充实,就要防备它;敌人兵力强大,就要避开它;敌人气势汹汹,就要屈挠它;敌人辞卑慎行,就要骄纵它;敌人休整得好,就要劳累它;敌人内部团结,就要离间它。在敌人毫无防备之处发动进攻,在敌人意料不到之时采取行动。这是军事家指挥的奥妙,是不能预先呆板规定的。

开战之前就预计能够取得胜利的,是因为胜利的条件充分;开战之前就预计不能胜利

War is a game of deception. Therefore, feign incapability when in fact capable; feign inactivity when ready to strike; appear to be far away when actually nearby, and vice versa. When the enemy is greedy for gains, hand out a bait to lure him; when he is in disorder, attack and overcome him; when he boasts substantial strength, be doubly prepared against him; and when he is formidable, evade him. If he is given to anger, provoke him. If he is timid and careful, encourage his arrogance. If his forces are rested, wear them down. If he is united as one, divide him. Attack where he is least prepared. Take action when he least expects you.

Herein lies a strategist's subtlety of command which is impossible to codify in hard-and-fast rules beforehand.

He who makes full assessment of the situation at the prewar council meeting in the temple (*translator's note*: *an ancient Chinese practice*) is more likely to win. He who makes

【原文】

算不胜者,得算少也。多算胜,少算不胜,而况于无算乎!吾以此观之,胜负见矣。

【今译】

的,是因为胜利的条件不充分。筹划周密就能胜利,筹划疏漏就不能胜利,何况不作筹划呢!我们根据这些来进行观察,谁胜谁败就很清楚了。

insufficient assessment of the situation at this meeting is less likely to win. This being the case, what chance has he of winning if he makes no assessment at all? With my assessment method, I can forecast who is likely to emerge as victor.

作战篇

【原文】

孙子曰：凡用兵之法，驰车千驷，革车千乘，带甲十万，千里馈粮；则内外之费，宾客之用，胶漆之材，车甲之奉，日费千金，然后十万之师举矣。

其用战也胜，久则钝兵挫锐，攻城则力屈，

【今译】

孙子说：用兵作战的一般规律是，出动轻型战车千辆，重型兵车千辆，军队十万，还要千里运粮；那么，前方后方的费用、招待国宾使节的用度、胶漆器材的供应、车辆盔甲的维修，每天就要耗费千金，然后，十万军队才能出动。

用这样的军队去作战就要求速胜，旷日持久就会使武器装备耗损，部队锐气受挫，攻城就会使

Waging War

Sunzi said:

Generally, a war operation requires one thousand light chariots, as many heavy chariots and a hundred thousand armored soldiers with provisions enough to carry them a thousand *li*. What with the expenses at home and in the field, stipends for the entertainment of state guests and diplomatic envoys, the cost of materials such as glue and lacquer (*tr.* : *for maintenance of equipment*) and sums spent for the maintenance of chariots and amour, the total expenditure will amount to one thousand pieces of gold a day. Only after all this money is in hand can an army of one hundred thousand men be raised.

In a war which involves such a huge army, the main objective should be quick victory. If the war is prolonged, the weapons will be blunted

【原文】

久暴师则国用不足。夫钝兵挫锐、屈力殚货,则诸侯乘其弊而起,虽有智者,不能善其后矣。故兵闻拙速,未睹巧之久也。夫兵久而国利者,未之有也。故不尽知用兵之害者,则不能尽知用兵之利也。

善用兵者,役不再籍,粮不三载;取用于国,因粮于敌,故军食可足也。

【今译】

战斗力耗尽。军队长期在外作战,就会使国家的财政发生困难,武器装备耗损,军队锐气挫伤,军事实力耗尽,国家经济枯竭,那么诸侯就会乘此危机发起进攻,到那时,即使有智谋高超的人,也无法挽回危局了。所以,用兵作战,只听说指挥虽拙但求速胜,而没有见过为讲究指挥工巧而求持久的。战争久拖不决而对国家有利的情形是没有的。所以,不完全了解用兵有害方面的人,就不能完全了解用兵的有利方面。

善于用兵的人,兵员不再次征集,粮秣不多次运输;武器装备自国内取用,粮食饲料在敌国补充。这样,军队的粮秣供应就充足了。

and the men's morale will be dampened. When they storm cities, their strength will be exhausted. Protracted campaigns will be a serious strain on the treasury. Now, when your weapons are blunted, your morale dampened, your strength exhausted and your treasury spent, neighbouring states will take advantage of your distress to strike. In that case, no one, however wise, will be able to avert the disastrous consequences which ensue.

Thus, while we have heard of blundering in seeking swift decisions in war, we have yet to see a smart operation that drags on endlessly. For there has never been a prolonged war from which a country has benefited. Those who are not fully aware of the harm in waging war are equally unable to understand fully the method of conducting war advantageously.

Those adept in waging war do not require a second conscription or replenishment of provisions from the home country. They obtain their military supplies from home but commandeer provisions from the enemy territory. Thus their army will always be plentifully supplied. When

【原文】

国之贫于师者远输,远输则百姓贫。近于师者贵卖,贵卖则百姓财竭,财竭则急于丘役。力屈、财殚,中原内虚于家。百姓之费,十去其七;公家之费,破车罢马,甲胄矢弩,戟楯蔽橹,丘牛大车,十去其六。

故智将务食于敌。食敌一钟,当吾二十钟;蒽秆一石,当吾二十石。

故杀敌者,怒也;取敌之利者,货也。

【今译】

国家之所以会因为用兵而贫穷,就是由于远道运输。远道运输,百姓就会贫穷。靠近军队集结的地方,物价就会上涨。物价上涨,就会使得百姓财富枯竭。财富枯竭,就要急于增加赋役。军力耗尽,财富枯竭,国内家家空虚,百姓的财产要耗去十分之七;国家的资财,也由于车辆损坏,马匹疲病,盔甲、箭弩、戟盾、大盾牌以及运输用的民间的牛和大车的征集、补充而损失十分之六。

所以,明智的将帅务求取粮于敌国。消耗敌国粮食一钟,等于从本国运送二十钟;动用敌国草料一石,等于从本国运送二十石。

要使士卒勇敢杀敌,就要激励部队的士气;要夺取敌人的物资,就要用财物作奖励。

a country is impoverished by military operations, it is because of the long distance transportation involved. Transporting supplies over long distances render the people destitute. Proximity of an army causes prices to go up, and high prices are a drain on the people's resources. When the resources are exhausted, exactions and levies are bound to increase. With military strength thus depleted and wealth consumed, the people's homes will be stripped bare. Seventy percent of the people's income is dissipated and sixty percent of the government's revenue goes to pay for maintenance of broken down chariots, worn-out horses, amour and helmets, arrows and crossbows, halberds and bucklers, spears and shields, draught oxen and heavy wagons.

Therefore, a wise general does his best to feed his troops on the enemy's grain, for one *zhong* (*tr*. *1,000 litres*) of grain obtained from enemy territory is equivalent to 20 *zhong* shipped from home country, and one *dan* (*tr*.: *60 kilos*) of fodder from enemy territory to 20 *dan* from home.

In order to embolden your men to annihilate the enemy, you must boost their morale; in order to encourage your men to seize enemy

【原文】

故车战得车十乘已上,赏其先得者,而更其旌旗,车杂而乘之,卒善而养之,是谓胜敌而益强。

故兵贵胜,不贵久。

故知兵之将,生民之司命,国家安危之主也。

【今译】

所以在车战中,凡缴获战车十辆以上的,就要奖励首先夺得战车的人,并把敌人的旗帜换成我军的旗帜,与我军的战车混合编组,对俘虏的兵卒要优待和使用他们,这就是所谓愈战胜敌人就愈是增强自己。

所以用兵贵在速胜,而不宜旷日持久。

所以懂得用兵作战的将帅,是民众生死的掌握者,是国家安危的主宰。

provisions, you must give them material rewards. Therefore, in a chariot battle, when more than ten chariots have been captured, reward those who captured the first one and replace the enemy banners and flags with your own. The captured chariots should be used together with yours. Prisoners of war should be treated kindly and taken into your ranks. This is what is meant by boosting one's own strength in the process of overpowering the enemy.

So, what is important in war is quick victory, not prolonged operations.

Thus, the commander who knows how to conduct a war is the arbiter of the people's fate, the man on whom the nation's security depends.

谋攻篇

【原文】

孙子曰：凡用兵之法，全国为上，破国次之；全军为上，破军次之；全旅为上，破旅次之；全卒为上，破卒次之；全伍为上，破伍次之。是故百战百胜，非善之善者也；不战而屈人之兵，善之善者也。

【今译】

孙子说：指导战争的法则是，使敌国完整地降服是上策，击破敌国就次一等；使敌人全"军"完整地降服是上策，击破它的"军"就次一等；使敌人全"旅"完整地降服是上策，击破它的"旅"就次一等；使敌人全"卒"完整地降服是上策，击破它的"卒"就次一等；使敌人全"伍"完整地降服是上策，击破它的"伍"就次一等。因此，百战百胜还不算高明中最高明的；不经交战而使敌人屈服，才算是高明中最高明的。

Attacking by Stratagem

Sunzi said:

Generally in war, the best policy is to take the enemy state whole and intact; to destroy it is not. To have the enemy's army surrender in its entirety is better than to crush it; likewise, to take a battalion, a company or a five-man squad intact is better than to destroy it. Therefore, to fight a hundred battles and win each and every one of them is not the wisest thing to do. To break the enemy's resistance without fighting is.

【原文】

故上兵伐谋,其次伐交,其次伐兵,其下攻城。攻城之法为不得已。修橹辒辌,具器械,三月而后成,距闉,又三月而后已。将不胜其忿而蚁附之,杀士三分之一而城不拔者,此攻之灾也。

故善用兵者,屈人之兵而非战也,拔人之城而非攻也,毁人之国而非久也,必以全争于天下,故兵不顿而利可全,此谋攻之法也。

【今译】

所以,上策是挫败敌人的战略计谋,其次是挫败敌人的外交,再次是战胜敌人的军队,下策是攻打敌人的城池。攻城的办法是不得已的。制造攻城用的巢车和四轮攻城车,准备攻城器械,三个月才能完成,构筑攻城的土山又要三个月才能完工。将帅抑制不住焦躁忿怒的情绪,指挥士卒像蚂蚁一样去爬梯攻城,士兵伤亡三分之一,而城还是攻不下,这就是攻城的危害。

所以,善于用兵的人,使敌人屈服而不靠直接交战,夺取敌人的城堡而不靠硬攻,毁灭敌人的国家而不需旷日久战,一定要用全胜的战略争胜于天下,这样,军队不疲惫受挫而胜利却可完满取得。这就是以计谋攻取敌人的法则。

Thus, the best policy in war is to thwart the enemy's strategy. The second best is to disrupt his alliances through diplomatic means. The third best is to attack his army in the field. The worst policy of all is to attack walled cities.

Attack a walled city only when there is no alternative. For it takes at least three months to get the mantlets and shielded vehicles ready and prepare the necessary arms and equipment; for it takes another three months to build the earthen mounds for soldiers to ascend the walls. The commander who loses his patience orders his troops to assault like swarming ants, with the result that one third of his men are slain and the city remains untaken. Such is the calamity of attacking walled cities.

Therefore, he who is skilled in war subdues the enemy without fighting. He captures the enemy's cities without assaulting them. He overthrows the enemy kingdom without prolonged operations in the field. By taking all under heaven with his "whole and intact strategy," he wins total victory without wearing out his troops. This is the method of attacking by stratagem.

【原文】

故用兵之法，十则围之，五则攻之，倍则分之，敌则能战之，少则能逃之，不若则能避之。

故小敌之坚，大敌之擒也。

夫将者，国之辅也，辅周则国必强，辅隙则国必弱。

故君之所以患于军者三：

不知军之不可以进而谓之进，不知军之不可以退而谓之退，是谓縻军。

【今译】

所以，用兵的法则是，有十倍于敌的兵力就包围它，有五倍于敌的兵力就进攻它，有两倍于敌的兵力就分散它，与敌人兵力相等就抗击它，兵力少于敌人就要退却，实力比敌人弱就要避免决战。所以，弱小的军队如果只知硬拼坚守，就会成为强大敌人的俘虏。

将帅是国家的辅佐，辅助周密，国家就强盛；辅助有缺陷，国家就会衰弱。

国君危害军队的情况有三种：

不了解军队不可以前进而命令它前进，不了解军队不可以后退而命令它后退，这叫束缚军队。

Consequently, the art of using troops is: when you outnumber the enemy ten to one, surround him; when five to one, attack him; when two to one, divide him; and if equally matched, stand up to him. (*tr*.: *Anotherversion of the text reads "when two to one, stand up to him; and if equally matched, divide him."*) If you are fewer than the enemy in number, retreat. If you are no match for him, try to elude him. For no matter how stubbornly a small force may fight, it must in the end succumb to greater strength and fall captive to it.

The commander is the country's bulwark. His proficiency in war can make the country strong, his deficiency makes it weak.

There are three ways by which a sovereign may bring disaster to his army:

One, he arbitrarily orders his army to advance or retreat when in fact it should not, thus hampering the initiative of the army.

【原文】

不知三军之事而同三军之政者,则军士惑矣。

不知三军之权而同三军之任,则军士疑矣。

三军既惑且疑,则诸侯之难至矣,是谓乱军引胜。

故知胜有五:

知可以战与不可以战者胜;

识众寡之用者胜;

上下同欲者胜;

【今译】

不了解军队的内部事务而主持军队的行政管理,将士就会迷惑。

不懂得军队的权谋而干预军队的指挥,将士就会疑虑。

军队既迷惑又疑虑,那么,各诸侯国乘机侵犯的灾难就来到了。这就叫做扰乱自己的军队而致使敌人获得胜利。

预知胜利有五个方面:

知道可以打或不可以打的,能胜利;

懂得兵多与兵寡的不同用法的,能胜利;

军队上下意愿一致的,能胜利;

Two, he interferes with the administration of the army when he is ignorant of its internal affairs, thus causing confusion among the officers and men.

Three, he interferes with the officers' command, unaware of the principle that an army should adopt different tactics according to different circumstances. This will create misgivings in the minds of the officers and men.

When an army is confused and fraught with misgivings, neighboring states will take advantage of the situation and attack. This will disrupt the army and help the enemy to win.

Therefore, there are five factors to consider in anticipating which side will win, namely:

The side which knows when to fight and when not to will win;

The side which knows the difference between commanding a large army and a small army will win;

The side which has unity of purpose among its officers and men will win;

【原文】

以虞待不虞者胜；

将能而君不御者胜。

此五者，知胜之道也。

故曰：知彼知己者，百战不殆；不知彼而知己，一胜一负；不知彼，不知己，每战必殆。

【今译】

以有准备对待无准备的，能胜利；

将帅有指挥能力而国君不加牵制的，能胜利。

这五条，是预知胜利的方法。

所以说，了解敌人又了解自己，百战都不会有危险；不了解敌人但了解自己，可能胜利也可能失败；不了解敌人也不了解自己，那就每战都必定有危险。

The side which engages enemy troops that are unprepared with preparedness on its own part will win; and

The side which has a capable commander who is free of interference from the sovereign will win.

Bearing these points in mind, one is able to forecast victory in a war.

Therefore I say: Know your enemy and know yourself and you can fight a hundred battles without peril. If you are ignorant of the enemy and know only yourself, you will stand equal chances of winning and losing. If you know neither the enemy nor yourself, you are bound to be defeated in every battle.

形　篇

　　孙子曰:昔之善战者,先为不可胜,以待敌之可胜。不可胜在己,可胜在敌。故善战者,能为不可胜,不能使敌之可胜。故曰:胜可知而不可为。

　　不可胜者,守也;可胜者,攻也。守则不

　　孙子说:从前善于指挥作战的人,先要做到不会被敌人战胜,以等待机会战胜敌人。不被敌人战胜的主动权在自己,能够战胜敌人则在于敌人有疏漏。所以,善于指挥作战的人,能够做到自己不会被战胜,而不能做到使敌人一定被战胜。所以说:胜利可以预见,但不能强求。

　　要不被敌人战胜,就要进行防御;要战胜敌人,就要采取进攻。采取防御是因为兵力不

Disposition (*xing* 形)

Sunzi said:

The skilled commanders of the past first
made themselves invulnerable, then waited for
the enemy's moment of vulnerability. Invulnerability depends on one's own efforts, whereas
victory over the enemy depends on the latter's
negligence. It follows that those skilled in warfare can make themselves invincible but they
cannot be sure of victory over the enemy.
Therefore it is said that victory can be anticipat-
ed but it cannot be forced.

Invulnerability lies with defense, and opportunity of victory with attack. One defends when
his strength is inadequate; he attacks when his

【原文】

足,攻则有余。善守者,藏于九地之下;善攻者,动于九天之上,故能自保而全胜也。

　　见胜不过众人之所知,非善之善者也;战胜而天下曰善,非善之善者也。故举秋毫不为多力,见日月不为明目,闻雷霆不为聪耳。古之所谓善战者,胜于易胜者也。故善战者之胜也,无智名,无勇功。故其战胜不忒,不

【今译】

足,采取进攻是因为兵力有余。善于防御的人,如隐蔽于极深的地下;善于进攻的人,如行动于极高的天上。所以,既能保全自己又能取得完全的胜利。

　　预见胜利不超过一般人的认识,不算高明中最高明的;经过激战取得胜利,普天下都说好,也算不得高明中最高明的。这就好比举得起秋毫算不上力大,看得见日月算不上眼明,听得见雷霆算不上耳聪一样。古时候所谓善于指挥作战的人的胜利,都是战胜容易战胜的敌人。所以,善于指挥作战的人所打的胜仗,没有智慧的名声,没有勇武的战功。他的战胜是不会有差错的。

strength is abundant. He who is skilled in defense positions his forces in places as safe and inaccessible as in the depth of the earth, whereas he who is skilled in attack strikes as from the highest reaches of heaven. In this way he is able both to protect himself and to win complete victory.

To foresee a victory which is within the ken of the ordinary people is not the acme of excellence. Neither is it the acme of excellence when one is acclaimed universally for winning a fierce battle. It is like lifting a strand of animal hair in autumn (*tr.*: *Animal hair is very fine and light in autumn.*), which is no sign of strength; like being able to see the sun and the moon, which is no test of vision; like hearing a thunderclap, which is no indication of hearing ability. What the ancients called a master of war is one who overpowers an enemy easy to defeat. The victories won by a master of war gain him neither fame for his wisdom nor merit

【原文】

忒者,其所措必胜,胜已败者也。故善战者,立于不败之地,而不失敌之败也。是故胜兵先胜而后求战,败兵先战而后求胜。善用兵者,修道而保法,故能为胜败之政。

兵法:一曰度,二曰量,三曰数,四曰称,五曰胜。地生度,度生量,量生数,数生称,称生

【今译】

其所以没有差错,是因为他的作战措施建立在必胜的基础上,战胜的是已处于失败地位的敌人。所以,善于指挥作战的人,总是使自己立于不败之地,而又不放过击败敌人的机会。因此,胜利的军队总是先有了胜利的把握而后才同敌人交战,失败的军队则是先同敌人交战而后企求取胜。善于指导战争的人,必须修明政治,确保法制,所以能够掌握胜败的主动权。

《兵法》说:一是度,二是量,三是数,四是称,五是胜。敌我所处地域的不同,产生双方土地面积大小不同的"度";"度"的不同,产生双方物产资源多少不同的"量";"量"的不同,产生双方兵员多寡不同的"数";"数"的不同,产生双方军事实力强弱不同的"称";"称"的不

for his valor, because he is bound to win as his tactics are built on assurances of victory. He defeats an enemy already defeated. Thus, the skilled warrior puts himself in a position in which he cannot be defeated and misses no opportunity to defeat his enemy.

So it is that a victorious army will not engage the enemy unless it is assured of the necessary conditions for victory, whereas an army destined to defeat rushes into battle in the hope that it will win by luck. The skilled warrior seeks victory by cultivating the way and strengthening rules and regulations, and in so doing, gains the initiative over his enemy.

The five elements mentioned in *The Rules of War* are: 1) measurement of space, 2) estimation of quantity, 3) calculation of number, 4) comparison of strength, and 5) assessment of chances of victory. Measurement of space refers to the difference in the territories of the opposing parties; from that derives estimation of quantity, which refers to the difference in resources; from that, calculation of numbers, which refers to the difference in the size of their troops; from that, comparison of the relative strengths of their armies and finally, assessment of the material base for the chances of victory.

【原文】

胜。故胜兵若以镒称铢，败兵若以铢称镒。胜者之战民也，若决积水于千仞之谿者，形也。

【今译】

同，最终决定战争的胜负成败。胜利的军队较之于失败的军队，就像用"镒"称"铢"那样占绝对优势；失败的军队较之于胜利的军队，就像用"铢"称"镒"那样处于绝对劣势。胜利者指挥作战，就像在八百丈高处决开溪中积水一样，这就是军事实力的"形"。

Thus, a victorious army has full advantage over its enemy, just like pitting 500 grains against one grain; the opposite is true with an army doomed to defeat, like pitting one against 500. So great is the disparity of strength that a victorious army goes into battle with the force of an onrushing torrent which, when suddenly released, plunges into a chasm a thousand fathoms deep. This is what we mean by disposition.

势　篇

【原文】

孙子曰：凡治众如治寡，分数是也；斗众如
斗寡，形名是也；三军之众，可使必受敌而无败
者，奇正是也；兵之所加，如以碫投卵者，虚实
是也。

凡战者，以正合，以奇胜。故善出奇者，无

【今译】

孙子说：管理大部队如同管理小部队一
样，这是军队的组织编制问题；指挥大部队作
战如同指挥小部队作战一样，这是指挥号令问
题；统帅全军，能够一旦遭到敌人进攻而不失
败的，这是"奇正"的战术变化问题；军队进攻
敌人，如同以石击卵一样，这是"避实击虚"的
正确运用问题。

作战都是用"正兵"当敌，用"奇兵"取胜。
所以善于出奇制胜的将帅，其战法变化就像天

Momentum (*shi* 势)

Sunzi said:

There is no difference between administering many troops and few troops. It is a matter of organization, of instituting layers of control. There is no difference between commanding a large army and a small one. It is a matter of communications, of establishing an efficient system of command signals. Thanks to the combined use of *qi* (奇) and *zheng* (正) tactics, the army is able to withstand the onslaught of the enemy forces. By staying clear of the enemy's strong points and striking at his weak points, it is able to fall upon the enemy like using a whetstone to crush an egg.

Generally, in battle, use *zheng* to engage the enemy and use *qi* to score victory. The resourcefulness of those skilled in the use of *qi* is as

【原文】

穷如天地,不竭如江河。终而复始,日月是也。死而复生,四时是也。声不过五,五声之变,不可胜听也。色不过五,五色之变,不可胜观也。味不过五,五味之变,不可胜尝也。战势不过奇正,奇正之变,不可胜穷也。奇正相生,如循环之无端,孰能穷之?

激水之疾,至于漂石者,势也;鸷鸟之疾,至于毁折者,节也。是故善战者,其势险,其节

【今译】

地那样不可穷尽,像江河那样永不枯竭。入而复出,是日月的运行;去而又来,是四季的更迭。乐音不过五个,然而五音的变化就听不胜听;颜色不过五种,然而五色的变化就看不胜看;滋味不过五味,然而五味的变化就尝不胜尝;作战的战术不过"奇""正",然而"奇正"的变化就无穷无尽。"奇""正"互相转化,就像顺着圆环旋转一样,无首无尾,谁能穷尽它呢?

湍急的流水飞快地奔泻,以致能漂移石头,这就是"势"。雄鹰迅飞搏击,以致能捕杀鸟兽,这就是"节"。所以善于指挥作战的人,进攻时态势险峻,冲锋时节奏急促。险峻的态

inexhaustible as heaven and earth and as unending as the flow of rivers; it is like the sun and the moon which end their course only to begin anew, like the four seasons which pass only to return once more. There are no more than five tones in music, yet their combinations give rise to countless melodies. There are no more than five primary colors, yet in combination, they produce innumerable hues. There are no more than five flavors, yet their blends produce endless varieties. In military tactics, there are only two types of operation, *qi* and *zheng*, yet their variations are limitless. They constantly change from one to the other, like moving in a circle with neither a beginning nor an end. Who can exhaust their possibilities?

When torrential water moves boulders, it is because of its momentum. When falcons strike and destroy their prey, it is because of perfect timing. Thus, when launching an offensive, a good commander creates a good posture which provides him with an irresistible momentum and

【原文】

短。势如彍弩，节如发机。

纷纷纭纭，斗乱而不可乱也；浑浑沌沌，形圆而不可败也。乱生于治，怯生于勇，弱生于强。治乱，数也；勇怯，势也；强弱，形也。故善动敌者，形之，敌必从之；予之，敌必取之。以利动之，以卒待之。

【今译】

势就像张满的弓弩，急促的节奏就像击发的弩机。

旌旗纷纷，人马纭纭，在混乱状态中作战而指挥不乱；浑浑沌沌，迷迷蒙蒙，在复杂形势下布阵而不会失败。示敌混乱，是因为有严整的组织；示敌怯懦，是因为有勇敢的素质；示敌弱小，是因为有强大的兵力。严整、混乱，这是组织编制的问题；勇敢、怯懦，这是态势好坏的问题；强大、弱小，这是实力大小的问题。所以，善于调动敌人的将帅，用假象迷惑敌人，敌人就会听从调动；用小利引诱敌人，敌人就会来夺取。用小利调动敌人，用重兵伺机击败敌人。

when he attacks, it is with lightning speed. The momentum is similar to that of a fully-drawn crossbow, the speed to that of the arrow leaving the bow.

Amidst the chaos of men and horses locked in battle beneath waving banners, there must be no disorder in command. The troops may appear to be milling about in circles, but they should be arrayed in a way that guarantees them against defeat. To simulate disorder, there must be strict organization. To simulate fear, there must be great courage. To simulate weakness, there must be strength. Order comes from organization, courage from momentum, and strength from disposition. Thus, those who are skilled in keeping the enemy on the move puzzle him with deceptive appearances according to which he will react. They lure the enemy with baits which he is certain to take. In so doing, they keep the enemy on the move and pounce on him at the right moment.

【原文】

故善战者,求之于势,不责于人,故能择人而任势。任势者,其战人也,如转木石。木石之性,安则静,危则动,方则止,圆则行。故善战人之势,如转圆石于千仞之山者,势也。

【今译】

所以善于指挥作战的人,总是去造成有利的态势,而不苛求部属,因此能选择适当的将帅去造成有利的态势。善于造成有利态势的将帅,他指挥部队作战,就像滚动木头、石头一样。木头、石头的特点是,放在安稳平坦的地方就静止,放在陡险的地方就滚动;方的静止不动,圆的滚动灵活。所以,善于指挥作战的人所造成的有利态势,就像转动圆石从八百丈的高山上滚下来一样。这就是"势"。

Therefore, one who is skilled at directing war always tries to turn the situation to his advantage rather than make excessive demands on his subordinates. Hence, he is able to select the right men and exploit the situation.

He who is skilful in turning the situation to his advantage can send his men into battle as he would roll logs or rocks. Logs and rocks remain immobile when they are on level ground, but roll forward when on a steep slope. The square ones do not move. The round ones roll with agility. Thus the strategic advantage of troops skillfully commanded in battle may be compared to the momentum of round boulders rolling down from mountain heights.

虚实篇

孙子曰:凡先处战地而待敌者佚,后处战地而趋战者劳。故善战者,致人而不致于人。

能使敌人自至者,利之也;能使敌人不得至者,害之也。故敌佚能劳之,饱能饥之,安能动之。出其所不趋,趋其所不意。行千里

【今译】

孙子说:凡先到达战场迎战敌人的就安逸从容,后到达战场仓促应战的就疲劳被动。所以善于指挥作战的人,能调动敌人而不被敌人调动。

能使敌人自动进到我预定地域的,是用小利引诱的结果;能使敌人不能进入我防区范围的,是制造困难阻止的结果。所以敌人休息得好,能够使它疲劳;敌人粮食充足,能够使它饥饿;敌人驻扎安稳,能够使它移动。出兵指向敌人无法援救的地方,行动于敌人

Weaknesses and Strengths
(*xu shi* 虚实)

Sunzi said:

Generally, he who first occupies the field of battle and awaits his enemy is rested and prepared; he who comes late to the scene and hastens into battle is weary and passive. Therefore, those skilled in war move the enemy rather than being moved by him.

Those who are able to make the enemy come voluntarily to the designated place do so by offering him some gain. And those who are able to keep him from coming do so by creating obstacles and inflicting damage on him. Thus, when the enemy is rested, tire him; when well fed, starve him; and when settled, get him on the move. All this is possible because you ap pear at places the enemy cannot come to the

【原文】

而不劳者,行于无人之地也;攻而必取者,攻其
所不守也;守而必固者,守其所不攻也。

故善攻者,敌不知其所守;善守者,敌不知
其所攻。微乎微乎,至于无形,神乎神乎,至于
无声,故能为敌之司命。进而不可御者,冲
其虚也;退而不可追者,速而不可及也。故
我欲战,敌虽高垒深沟,不得不与我战者,攻

【今译】

意料不到的方向。行军千里而不疲劳,因为走
的是没有敌人阻碍的地区;进攻而必然得手,
因为进攻的是敌人不防守的地方;防御而必然
能稳固,因为扼守的正是敌人不易攻克的地
方。

所以善于进攻的,使敌人不知道怎么防
守;善于防御的,使敌人不知道怎么进攻。微
妙呀,微妙到看不出形迹;神奇呀,神奇到听不
到声息,所以能成为敌人的主宰。前进而使敌
人不能抵御的,是因为冲向敌人空虚的地
方;后退而使敌人无法追击的,是因为行动
迅速追赶不上。所以,我军要打,敌人即使
高垒深沟也不得不脱离阵地与我作战,是因为

rescue of and least expects you. That you may march a thousand *li* without tiring yourself is because you are passing through territory where there is no enemy to stop you. That you are certain to take what you attack is because you attack a place the enemy cannot protect. That you are certain of success in holding what you defend is because you defend a place the enemy finds impregnable.

Therefore, against the expert in attack, the enemy does not know where to defend; and against the expert in defense, the enemy does not know where to attack. So subtle is the expert that he leaves no trace, so mysterious that he makes no sound. Thus, he becomes the arbiter of his enemy's fate. His advance is irresistible because he plunges into his enemy's weak position; and his withdrawal cannot be overtaken because it is so swift. Thus, when we wish to give battle, the enemy cannot but leave his position to engage us even though he is safe behind high walls and deep moats, because we attack a position he must rescue. When we wish

【原文】

其所必救也;我不欲战,画地而守之,敌不得与
我战者,乖其所之也。

故形人而我无形,则我专而敌分;我专为
一,敌分为十,是以十攻其一也,则我众而敌
寡;能以众击寡者,则吾之所与战者约矣。吾
所与战之地不可知,

不可知,则敌所备者多;敌所备者多,则
吾所与战者寡矣。故备前则后寡,备后则前

【今译】

进攻的是敌人必救的地方;我军不想打,虽然
布阵防守,敌人也无法来同我作战,是因为我
诱使敌人改变了预定的进攻方向。

所以,使敌情暴露而我情不露痕迹,我军
的兵力集中而敌人的兵力则分散;我军兵力集
中在一处,敌人兵力分散在十处,这是用十倍
于敌的兵力去攻击敌人,这样就我众敌寡;能
以众击寡,那么,我军与之作战的敌人就有限
了。我军所要进攻的地方敌人不得而知,

不得而知,那么所要防备的地方就多了;
敌人所要防备的地方多,那么我军与之作战
的敌人就少了。所以,防备了前面,后面的
兵力就薄弱;防备了后面,前面的兵力就薄弱;

to avoid battle, we may simply draw a line on the ground by way of defense and the enemy cannot engage us because we have diverted him to a different target.

Hence, if we are able to determine the enemy's disposition while concealing our own, then we can concentrate our forces while his are dispersed. And if our forces are concentrated at one place while his are scattered at ten places, then it is ten to one when we attack him at one place. This means we will be numerically superior. If we are able to use many to strike few at a selected point, those we deal with will be greatly reduced in number. The enemy must not know where we intend to give battle, for if he doesn't know where we intend to give battle, he must prepare in a great many places and, when he does that, those we have to fight in any one place will be few in number. Thus if the enemy makes preparations by reinforcing his front, his rear will be weakened; and if he makes preparations by reinforcing his rear, his front will be weakened. If he does this to defend his left,

【原文】

寡,备左则右寡,备右则左寡,无所不备,则无所不寡。寡者,备人者也;众者,使人备己者也。

故知战之地,知战之日,则可千里而会战。不知战地,不知战日,则左不能救右,右不能救左,前不能救后,后不能救前,而况远者数十里,近者数里乎? 以吾度之,越人之兵虽多,亦奚益于胜败哉? 故曰:胜可为也。敌虽众,可使无斗。

【今译】

防备了左边,右边的兵力就薄弱;防备了右边,左边的兵力就薄弱。无处不防备,就无处的兵力不薄弱。兵力薄弱,是因为处处去防备;兵力充足,是因为迫使敌人处处防备。

所以,能预知交战的地点、预知交战的时间,就可跋涉千里去同敌人作战。不能预知交战的地点、不能预知交战的时间,那么就左翼不能救右翼,右翼不能救左翼,前面不能救后面,后面不能救前面,何况远的数十里,近的数里呢? 依我看来,越国的兵力虽多,对争取战争的胜利又有什么补益呢? 所以说,胜利是可以造成的。敌军虽多,可以使它无法同我较量。

his right will be weakened; and if his right, his left will be weakened. To be prepared everywhere is to be weak everywhere. One who has to prepare against the enemy everywhere is bound to be weak; one who makes the enemy prepare against him everywhere is bound to be strong.

Therefore if one knows when and where a battle will be fought, his troops can march a thousand *li* to fight the enemy. But if one knows neither the battleground nor the date of battle, his left flank will not be able to rescue his right, nor the other way around. Similarly his front will not be able to support his rear, and vice versa. How much more so if his reinforcements are scores of *li* away, and even the closest are separated by several *li*! In my view, while the troops of Yue (*tr.: a neighboring state of Wu*) are numerous, that alone does not determine the outcome of war. Therefore, I say: victory can be created. Even if the enemy is numerically stronger, we can render it impotent.

【原文】

故策之而知得失之计,作之而知动静之理,形之而知死生之地,角之而知有余不足之处。故形兵之极,至于无形;无形,则深间不能窥,智者不能谋。因形而错胜于众,众不能知;人皆知我所以胜之形,而莫知吾所以制胜之形。故其战胜不复,而应形于无穷。

【今译】

所以,分析敌情以了解敌人作战计划的优劣,挑动敌军以了解敌人的活动规律,佯动示形以了解敌人地形的有利不利,战斗侦察以了解敌人兵力部署的虚实强弱。因此,伪装到最好的地步,就看不出形迹;看不出形迹,那么即使有深藏的间谍也窥察不到我方的底细,聪明的敌人也想不出对付我方的办法。把根据敌情的变化而取得的胜利摆在众人面前,众人还是看不出其中的奥妙;人们都知道我方取胜的方法,但不知道我方是怎样用这些方法来取胜的。所以每次战胜都不是重复老一套战法,而是适应不同的情况,变化无穷。

So one must analyze the enemy's plan in order to have a clear understanding of his strong and weak points. Provoke the enemy into action so as to ascertain his pattern of movement. Lure him into the open so as to find out the vulnerable spots in his disposition. Probe him so as to learn where his strength is abundant and where deficient. Now the ultimate in troop disposition is to leave no trace of how they are disposed. In this way, even the cleverest spy cannot detect anything, nor can the best brains succeed in scheming against us. Even if we show people the flexible tactics we used to gain victory in conformity with the changing enemy situation, they still cannot comprehend them. The enemy may know the tactics by which we win, but he does not know how we use the tactics to defeat him. Following each victory, we do not repeat the same tactics. We change them constantly to suit the changing circumstances.

【原文】

夫兵形象水,水之形,避高而趋下;兵之形,避实而击虚。水因地而制流,兵因敌而制胜。故兵无常势,水无常形。能因敌变化而取胜者,谓之神。故五行无常胜,四时无常位,日有短长,月有死生。

【今译】

用兵的规律好像水的流动,水的流动是避开高处而流向低处;作战的规律是避开敌人雄厚的实力而攻击它的弱点。水因地势的高低而制约流向,作战则根据敌人的变化而夺取胜利。战争没有固定的态势,水流没有不变的形态。能根据敌情的变化而夺取胜利的,就叫做用兵如神。五行没有哪一个固定独胜,四季没有哪一个固定不变,白昼有短有长,月亮有缺有圆。

Now the law governing military operations is as that governing the flow of water, which always evades high points, choosing lower ones instead. To operate the army successfully, we must avoid the enemy's strong points and seek out his weak points. As the water changes its course in accordance with the contours of the terrain, so a warrior changes his tactics in accordance with the enemy's changing situation. There is no fixed pattern in the use of tactics in war, just as there is no constant course in the flow of water. He who wins modifies his tactics in accordance with the changing enemy situation and this works miracles.

None of the five elements of nature (*wuxing* 五行) is ever predominant, and none of the four seasons lasts forever. Some days are longer and some shorter. The moon waxes and wanes.

军争篇

孙子曰：凡用兵之法，将受命于君，合军聚众，交和而舍，莫难于军争。军争之难者，以迂为直，以患为利。故迂其途，而诱之以利，后人发，先人至，此知迂直之计者也。

故军争为利，军争为危。举军而争利，则

孙子说：大凡用兵的法则，将帅接受国君的命令，从组织军队、聚集军需到同敌人对阵，没有比两军争利更困难的。两军争利最困难的，是要把迂回的道路变为直路，把困难变为有利。所以要迂回绕道，并用小利引诱敌人，这样就能后于敌人出发，却先于敌人到达要争夺的要地，这就是懂得以迂为直的方法了。

所以两军争利有利，两军争利也有危险。带着全部装备辎重去争利，就不能按时到达

58

Contest to Gain the
Initiative

Sunzi said:

Generally in war, the commander receives his mandate from the sovereign. In the process of assembling his troops, mobilizing the population and taking up positions against the enemy, nothing is more difficult than troop maneuvering to gain the initiative in war. What is involved here is to turn the tortuous into the direct and to turn adversity into advantage. You render the enemy's route tortuous by luring him with inducements of easy gains, and as a result, you may set out after he does but arrive at the contested battlefield before him. To be able to do so is to have understood the method of turning the tortuous into the direct.

Troop maneuvering can be a source of both advantage and disaster. If you throw in the army with all its equipment and supplies to cont-

【原文】

不及；委军而争利，则辎重捐。是故卷甲而趋，日夜不处，倍道兼行，百里而争利，则擒三将军，劲者先，疲者后，其法十一而至；五十里而争利，则蹶上将军，其法半至；三十里而争利，则三分之二至。是故军无辎重则亡，无粮食则亡，无委积则亡。

故不知诸侯之谋者，不能豫交；不知山林、

【今译】

预定地域；放下装备辎重去争利，装备辎重就会损失。因此，卷甲急进，昼夜不停，加倍行程强行军，走上百里去争利，三军将领可能被俘，强壮的士卒先到，疲弱的士卒掉队，这种作法只会有十分之一的兵力赶到；走五十里去争利，先头部队的将领会受挫折，这种作法只有半数兵力赶到；走三十里去争利，就只有三分之二的兵力赶到。所以，军队没有辎重就不能生存，没有粮食就不能生存，没有物资储备就不能生存。

所以不了解列国诸侯的战略企图，不能与其结交；不了解山林、险阻、水路沼泽等地形，

end for some advantage, you will not arrive in time; if you abandon them, your equipment and supplies will be lost. For this reason, if an army stores away its amour and sets off in haste, not stopping for days and nights and marching at double speed for 100 *li* to gain the advantage, some of its generals might be captured by the enemy, its strongest men might get there first but the exhausted ones would lag behind, and in that case, only one tenth of the army would reach the destination. In a forced march of 50 *li* to contend for advantage, the commander of the advance unit might be defeated, and as a rule only half of the army would reach its destination. But were it to travel 30 *li* at such a pace to contend for advantage, then two-thirds of the army would reach its destination. It must be remembered that an army which is without its equipment, food and fodder, and material reserves cannot survive.

Unless you know the strategic intentions of the rulers of the neighboring states, you cannot enter into alliances with them; unless you know the lay of the land — its mountains and forests, its natural hazards, its rivers and marshes — you

【原文】

险阻、沮泽之形者,不能行军;不用乡导者,不能得地利。故兵以诈立,以利动,以分合为变者也。故其疾如风,其徐如林,侵掠如火,不动如山,难知如阴,动如雷震;掠乡分众,廓地分利,悬权而动。先知迂直之计者胜。此军争之法也。

《军政》曰:"言不相闻,故为金鼓;视不相见,故为旌旗。"夫金鼓旌旗者,所以一人之耳

【今译】

不能行军;不使用向导,不能得地利。所以用兵打仗要依靠诡诈多变来取胜,根据是否有利来决定自己的行动,按照分散和集中来变化兵力的使用。所以,军队行动迅速时像疾风,舒缓时像森林,攻击时像烈火,防御时像山岳,荫蔽时像阴天,冲锋时像迅雷。掳掠乡邑,要分兵掠取;扩张领土,要分兵扼守;衡量利害然后决定行动。事先懂得以迂为直的方法就胜利。这就是两军争利的原则。

《军政》说:"因为用语言指挥听不到,所以设置金鼓;用动作指挥看不到,所以设置旌旗。"金鼓旌旗,是统一全军视听的。全军行

cannot maneuver your troops on it; unless you employ local guides, you cannot turn the terrain to your advantage.

Now war is a game of deception. Move when it is advantageous, and disperse and concentrate as necessary to bring about changes in the military situation advantageous to your forces. When the army advances, it is as swift as the wind; when it is immobile, as still as the forest; when it attacks, as destructive as a fire; when it defends, as immovable as the mountain; when it conceals itself, it is as though hidden behind an overcast sky; and when it strikes, it can be as sudden as a thunderbolt. When plundering the countryside, divide your forces; when extending your territory, distribute them to hold key points. Weigh the pros and cons before moving into action. He who masters the tactics of turning the tortuous into the direct will be the victor. That is the essence of the armed contest.

The Book of Military Administration states: "As oral commands cannot be heard in the din of battle, drums and gongs are used; as signal commands cannot be seen in battle, flags and banners are used." Drums, gongs, flags and banners are used to coordinate the sights and

【原文】

目也。人既专一,则勇者不得独进,怯者不得
独退,此用众之法也。故夜战多火鼓,昼战多
旌旗,所以变人之耳目也。

　　故三军可夺气,将军可夺心。是故朝气
锐,昼气惰,暮气归。故善用兵者,避其锐气,
击其惰归,此治气者也。以治待乱,以静待
哗,此治心者也。以近待远,以佚待劳,以饱

【今译】

动既然一致,那么勇敢的就不能单独前进,怯
懦的也不能单独后退,这就是指挥大部队作战
的方法。所以,夜间作战多用火光和鼓声,白
天作战多用旌旗。之所以变换这些信号都是
为了适应士卒的视听能力。

　　对于敌人的军队,可以打击它的士气;对于
敌人的将领,可以动摇他的决心。军队初战时士
气锐不可当,过一段时间就逐渐懈怠,最后就疲
乏衰竭了。所以善于用兵的人,要避开敌人的锐
气,等待敌人士气衰竭时再去打击它,这是掌
握军队士气的方法。以自己的严整对付敌人
的混乱,以自己的镇静对付敌人的轻躁,这是
掌握军队心理的方法。以自己部队的接近战场

hearing of the troops so that they will act as one, so that the brave will not have to advance alone, nor the timid retreat by themselves. This is the art of directing a large number of troops. That is why in night battles, torches and drums are widely used and in day battles, flags and banners. The alternating use of these signals helps communication with the soldiers.

An entire army can be demoralized and its general deprived of his presence of mind. At the beginning of a campaign, the soldiers' morale is high, after a while it begins to flag and in the end it is gone. Therefore, he who is skilled in war avoids the enemy when the latter's spirit is high, and strikes when his spirit drains. This is how he copes with the question of morale. In good order, he awaits a disorderly enemy; with calm, he awaits a clamorous enemy. This is how he copes with self-possession. Being close to the battlefield, he awaits an enemy coming from afar; well rested, he awaits an exhausted

【原文】

待饥,此治力者也。无邀正正之旗,勿击堂堂之陈,此治变者也。

故用兵之法,高陵勿向,背丘勿逆,佯北勿从,锐卒勿攻,饵兵勿食,归师勿遏,围师必阙,穷寇勿迫。此用兵之法也。

【今译】

对付敌人的远道而来,以自己部队的安逸休整对付敌人的奔走疲劳,以自己部队的饱食对付敌人的饥饿,这是掌握军队战斗力的方法。不要去拦击旗帜整齐部署周密的敌人,不要去攻击阵容堂皇实力强大的敌人,这是掌握机动变化的方法。

用兵的法则是:敌军占领山地不要去仰攻,敌军背靠高地不要正面迎击,敌军假装败退不要跟踪追击,敌军精锐不要去攻击,诱兵不要去理睬,退回本国的敌军不要去拦截,包围敌人要虚留缺口,濒临绝境的敌人不要过分逼迫。这就是用兵的法则。

enemy; with well-fed troops, he awaits hungry ones. This is how he copes with the question of strength. He does not intercept an enemy whose banners are in perfect array and refrains from attacking a powerful army in full formation. This is how he copes with changing circumstances.

When fighting a battle, do not launch an uphill attack on an enemy who occupies the high ground; do not fight an enemy that has his back to a hill; do not pursue an enemy that feigns retreat; do not attack his crack troops; do not swallow the enemy's bait; do not intercept an enemy returning home; in surrounding the enemy, leave him an escape route; do not press a cornered enemy. This is the art of employing troops.

九变篇

【原文】

孙子曰：凡用兵之法，将受命于君，合军聚众，圮地无舍，衢地交合，绝地无留，围地则谋，死地则战；涂有所不由，军有所不击，城有所不攻，地有所不争，君命有所不受。故将通于九变之地利者，知用兵矣；将不通于九变之

【今译】

孙子说：大凡用兵的法则，主将接受国君的命令，组织军队、聚集军需。出征时，在难于通行的地区不可宿营，在三国交界的地区应结交诸侯，在敌国控制的区域不可停留，在敌人可以以少击多的地方要巧设计谋，陷入只有拼命才能求生的地方就要坚决奋战。道路有些不要走，敌军有些不要打，城邑有些不要攻，土地有些不要争，国君的命令有些不要接受。将帅能够精通以上九种机变运用的，就是懂得用兵了；将帅不精通"九变"的运用，

Varying the Tactics
(*jiu bian* 九变)

Sunzi said:

Generally in war, the commander receives his mandate from the sovereign, assembles his troops and mobilizes the population for war. After he sets out, he should not encamp on difficult grounds; he should seek the support of neighboring states in border areas; he should not linger in enemy-occupied areas; he should have contingency plans when passing through the areas where the enemy is able to defeat a strong army with less troops; he should fight desperately with the enemy where there is no other way out. There are roads he should not take, armies he should not attack, walled cities he should not assault, territories he should not contest for and commands of the sovereign he should not obey.

Thus, a commander fully conversant with these variations of tactics will know how to employ his troops, while the one who is not, even if he knows the lay of the land, will not be able to use it to his advantage. A commander who

【原文】

利者,虽知地形,不能得地之利矣。治兵不知
九变之术,虽知五利,不能得人之用矣。

是故智者之虑,必杂于利害。杂于利而务
可信也;杂于害而患可解也。

是故屈诸侯者以害;役诸侯者以业;趋诸
侯者以利。

故用兵之法,无恃其不来,恃吾有以待也;

【今译】

虽然了解地形,也不能得到地利。指挥军队而
不懂得"九变"的方法,虽然知道"五利",也不
能充分发挥军队的作用。

聪明的将帅考虑问题,必须兼顾到利害两
个方面。在不利条件下要考虑到有利因素,大
事才可顺利完成;在顺利条件下要看到不利的
因素,祸患才能解除。

所以,制服诸侯是靠计谋伤害,役使诸侯
是靠实力威服,调动诸侯是靠小利引诱。

用兵的法则是,不要寄望于敌人不来,而
要依靠自己做好了充分的准备;不要寄望于敌

70

does not know the art of varying tactics will not be able to make the most of his army even if he knows the Five Advantages (*tr.*: *it is not apparent from the context what the Five Advantages are. Most commentators believe that they refer to the five " should nots" mentioned in the last sentence of the previous paragraph*).

For this reason, the wise commander or general, in his deliberations, will take into account both the favorable and the unfavorable factors. By considering the favorable factors when faced with difficulties, he will be able to accomplish great tasks. By considering the unfavorable factors when everything proceeds smoothly, he will be able to avoid possible disasters.

To subjugate the neighboring states, hit them where it hurts; to keep them occupied, make trouble for them; and to make them rush about, inveigle them with the prospects of ostensible gain.

Hence, it is a rule in war that you must not count on the enemy not coming, but always be

【原文】

无恃其不攻,恃吾有所不可攻也。

故将有五危:必死,可杀也;必生,可虏也;忿速,可侮也;廉洁,可辱也;爱民,可烦也。凡此五者,将之过也,用兵之灾也。覆军杀将,必以五危,不可不察也。

【今译】

人不进攻,而要依靠自己拥有力量使敌人无法进攻。

将帅有五种致命的弱点:只知死拼会被诱杀;贪生怕死会被俘虏;急躁易怒会中敌轻侮之计;廉洁好名过于自尊则不免受辱;一味爱民而不审度利害则会被动烦劳。这五种情况是将帅的过错,也是用兵的灾害。军队覆灭,将帅被杀,必定是因这五种危险引起的,不可不充分注意。

ready for him; that you must not count on the enemy not attacking, but make yourself so strong that you are invincible.

There are five weaknesses of character for a commander. If he is stubborn and reckless, he may be deceived and killed. If he fears death more than anything else, he may be captured. If he is hot tempered, he may be provoked. If he is honest but has too delicate a sense of honor, he is open to insult. If he is too compassionate towards his people, he may be easily troubled and upset. These five traits constitute serious faults for a commander, and can prove calamitous in his conduct of war. The destruction of the army and the death of its commander are invariably the consequences of these weaknesses which must not be overlooked under any circumstances.

行军篇

【原文】

孙子曰：凡处军相敌：绝山依谷，视生处高，战隆无登，此处山之军也。绝水必远水；客绝水而来，勿迎之于水内，令半济而击之，利；欲战者，无附于水而迎客；视生处高，无迎水流，此处水上之军也。绝斥泽，惟亟去无

【今译】

孙子说：在不同地形上处置军队和观察敌情，应该注意：通过山地，必须沿着有水草的山谷行进，在高而向阳的地方驻扎，敌人占领高地，不要仰攻，这是在山地对军队的处置。横渡江河，应远离流水驻扎；敌人渡水而来，不要迎击它于水内，让它渡过一半时去攻击它，才有利；如果要与敌决战，不要紧靠水边列阵迎敌；在江河地带扎营，也要居高向阳，不要面迎水流，这是在江河地带对军队的处置。通过盐碱沼泽地带，要迅速离开，不要停

Deploying the Troops

Sunzi said:

Generally, in positioning your troops and assessing the enemy, you should pay attention to the following:

While passing through mountains, stay close to the valleys and pitch camp on high ground facing the sun; if the enemy is on high ground, avoid fighting an uphill battle. So much for positioning an army when in the mountains.

After crossing a river, move to distance yourself from it; when the advancing enemy is crossing the river, do not meet him in the river; it is to your advantage to wait until he is halfway across and then strike; if you are ready for a decisive battle, do not position your troops near the water to confront your enemy; when encamping in such a region, take up a position on high ground facing the sun; do not take up a position that is downstream from the enemy. So much for positioning an army when near a river.

When crossing salt marshes, get through them

【原文】

留;若交军于斥泽之中,必依水草而背众树,此处斥泽之军也。平陆处易而右背高,前死后生,此处平陆之军也。凡此四军之利,黄帝之所以胜四帝也。

凡军好高而恶下,贵阳而贱阴,养生而处实,军无百疾,是谓必胜。丘陵堤防,必处其阳而右背之。此兵之利,地之助也。上雨,水沫

【今译】

留;如果同敌军遭遇于盐碱沼泽地带,就必须靠近水草而背靠树林。这是在盐碱沼泽地带对军队的处置。在平原上应占领开阔地域,而主要翼侧要依托高地,前低后高,这是在平原地带对军队的处置。以上四种"处军"原则的好处,就是黄帝所以能战胜四帝的原因。

凡是驻军总是喜欢干燥的高地而讨厌潮湿的洼地,重视向阳面而避开阴暗面,人马得以休养生息,军需供应充足,将士百病不生,这样就有了胜利的保证。在丘陵堤防地带,必须占领它向阳的一面,并把主要翼侧背靠着它。这些对于用兵有利的措施,是得自地形条件的辅助。上游下雨,洪水突至,要涉

quickly and without delay; if you encounter the enemy in the middle of a marshland, you must take a position close to reeds and water with trees to your rear. So much for positioning an army in marshland.

On flatlands, position yourself on open ground, with the main flank backed by high ground; that way the dangerous ground is in front of you and the safe ground is behind you. So much for positioning an army on flatlands.

It was such advantageous positioning of his troops in these four different situations that enabled the Yellow Emperor to defeat his four opponents.

Generally speaking, a maneuvering army prefers high, dry ground to low, wet ground; it prizes the sunny side and shuns the shady side, so that food and water would be readily available and remain in ample supply and men and horses may rest and restore their strength and be free of diseases. These conditions will guarantee victory.

When encountering hills, embankments and dikes, the army must be positioned on the sunny side with the main flank backed against the slope. These measures are beneficial because they help to exploit whatever the terrain affords.

When it is raining upstream and foaming waters

【原文】

至,欲涉者,待其定也。

　　凡地有绝涧、天井、天牢、天罗、天陷、天隙,必亟去之,勿近也。吾远之,敌近之;吾迎之,敌背之。军行有险阻、潢井、葭苇、山林蘙荟者,必谨复索之,此伏奸之所处也。

　　敌近而静者,恃其险也;远而挑战者,欲人之进也;其所居易者,利也。众树动者,来也;众草多障者,疑也;鸟起者,伏也;兽骇者,覆也。尘高而锐者,

【今译】

水,必须等水流平稳之后。

　　地形有"绝涧"、"天井"、"天牢"、"天罗"、"天陷"、"天隙",必须迅速离开,不要接近。我们应远离这种地形,让敌人去靠近它;我们应面向着它,让敌人背靠着它。军营两旁遇有隘路、湖沼、水网、芦苇、山林以及草木茂盛的地方,必须谨慎反复地搜索,这些都是奸细可能隐伏的地方。

　　敌人逼近而安静的,是仗它占领了险要地形;敌人离我方很远而来挑战的,是想引诱我方前进;敌人之所以驻扎在平坦的地方,是因为据有有利条件。许多树木摇动,是敌人隐蔽前来;草丛中有许多障碍,是敌人布下疑阵;群鸟惊飞,是下面有伏兵;野兽骇跑,是敌人大举突袭。尘土高而尖,是敌

descend, do not try to cross immediately; wait for the water to subside.

When you encounter steep river gorges, deep shafts, boxed-in recesses, tangled undergrowth, treacherous quagmires or dangerous crevasses, move away with haste. If possible, do not approach them. While you keep a distance from them, try to let the enemy get close to them; while you face them, let the enemy have his back to them.

Be on guard if the army is marching past precipitous ravines, marshes, reeds and rushes, forested hills and thick undergrowth. These places must be searched thoroughly, for they are where ambushes are laid and spies are hidden.

If the enemy is close at hand and yet remains quiet, he is relying on the natural strength of his position; if he is at a distance and yet provokes you, he is luring you to advance; if he positions himself on level ground, it is because he has some advantage.

If there is movement in the trees, it is the enemy coming stealthily; if there are many obstacles in the bushes, he is trying to confuse you; if birds take to flight, there must be an ambush; if animals are scurrying away in panic, the enemy is mounting a surprise attack; if the dust rises high,

【原文】

车来也;卑而广者,徒来也;散而条达者,樵采也;少而往来者,营军也。辞卑而益备者,进也;辞强而进驱者,退也;轻车先出居其侧者,陈也;无约而请和者,谋也;奔走而陈兵车者,期也;半进半退者,诱也。杖而立者,饥也;汲而先饮者,渴也;见利而不进者,劳也。鸟集者,虚也;夜呼者,恐也;军扰者,将不重也;旌

【今译】

人战车驶来;尘土低而宽广,是敌人的步兵开来;尘土疏散飞扬,是敌人在曳柴而行;尘土少而时起时落,是敌人正在扎营。敌人使者措词谦逊却又在加紧战备的,是准备进攻;措词诡诈而强硬做出前进姿态的,是准备后退;轻车先出动,部署在翼侧的,是在布列阵势;尚未受挫而来讲和的,是另有阴谋;兵卒奔走而布列兵车的,是期待与我决战;半退半进的,是企图引诱我军。敌兵倚着兵器站立,是因为饥饿;打水急于先饮,是因为干渴;见利而不前进,是因为疲劳。营寨上聚集鸟雀,是因为下面是空营;夜间惊叫,是因为恐慌;敌营惊扰纷乱,是因为将领无威严;旗帜摇动不齐,是因为

his chariots are coming; if the dust spreads out low on the ground, his foot soldiers are coming; if the dust reaches out in different directions, his units are out seeking firewood; if a few clouds of dust come and go, his camp is being made.

If his emissaries sound humble and yet he steps up his readiness for war, he plans to advance; if their language is belligerent and they put on an aggressive air, he plans to retreat; if his light chariots move out first and take up position on the flanks, he is moving into formation; if he has suffered no setback and yet sues for peace, that means he has something up his sleeves; if his troops move rapidly and his chariots are in formation, he is anticipating a decisive battle; if some of his troops advance and some retreat, he is seeking to lure you forward; if his soldiers are leaning on their weapons, they are hungry; if those sent to fetch water drink first, they are thirsty; if there is an advantage to be gained and yet they do not advance to take it, they are weary.

Where birds gather over the enemy camp, it is unoccupied; where there are shouts in the night, the enemy is frightened; where there are disturbances in the ranks, the enemy troops are

【原文】

旗动者,乱也;吏怒者,倦也;粟马肉食,军无悬
甀,不返其舍者,穷寇也。谆谆翕翕,徐与人言
者,失众也;数赏者,窘也;数罚者,困也;先暴而
后畏其众者,不精之至也;来委谢者,欲休息也。
兵怒而相迎,久而不合,又不相去,必谨察之。

兵非益多也,惟无武进,足以并力、料敌、取
人而已;夫惟无虑而易敌者,必擒于人。

【今译】

敌人队伍已经混乱;军官易怒,是因为全军疲倦
困乏;用粮食喂马,杀牲口吃肉,收拾起炊具,不
返回营舍的,是准备拼命突围的穷寇。低声下
气同部下讲话的,是因为敌将失去人心;不断犒
赏士卒的,是因为没有办法;不断惩罚部属的,
是因为处境困难;先强暴后又惧怕部下的,是因
为将领太不精明;派来的使者措词委婉、态度谦
逊的,是因为想休战。敌人愤怒向我前进,但久
不交锋又不撤退的,必须谨慎地观察它。

兵力并不是愈多愈好,只要不轻敌冒进,而
能集中兵力、判明敌情、取得部下信任,也就足
够了。那种既不深思熟虑又轻敌的人,必定会
被敌人俘虏。

in disorder; where his officers are easily angered, the enemy is exhausted; where the enemy feeds his horses grain and his men meat and his men put away their cooking pots and show no intention of returning to their camps, the enemy is desperate and is ready to force a breakthrough; where the enemy commander speaks to his subordinates in a meek and halting voice, he has lost their confidence; where he grants too many rewards, he has no alternative; where he metes out too many punishments, he is in dire straits; when the commander erupts violently at his subordinates only to be afraid of them later, he is totally inept; when the enemy's emissaries come with conciliatory words, he wants to end hostilities; but when an enemy confronts you angrily for a long time without either joining battle or leaving his position, then you must watch him with utmost care.

The strength of an army does not lie in mere numbers. Do not advance recklessly. So long as you can concentrate your own forces, have a clear picture of the enemy's situation and secure the full support of your men, that is sufficient. He who fails to give this careful consideration and takes his enemy lightly is certain to be captured by him.

【原文】

卒未亲附而罚之则不服，不服则难用也；卒已亲附而罚不行，则不可用也。故令之以文，齐之以武，是谓必取。令素行以教其民，则民服；令不素行以教其民，则民不服。令素行者，与众相得也。

【今译】

士卒还没有亲附就执行惩罚，他们就不服，不服就很难使用。士卒已经亲附，如果纪律仍不执行，也不能用来作战。所以要用怀柔的手段去笼络他们，用严格的手段去管束他们，这样就必定能取胜。平素能严格贯彻命令、管教兵卒，兵卒就服从；平素不严格贯彻命令、管教兵卒，兵卒就不服从。军令平素就有很高威信的，表明将帅同兵卒之间相处融洽。

If you punish soldiers for not being devoted to you, they will remain disobedient; and if they are disobedient, they will be difficult to use. But even when you have their devotion, if discipline is not enforced, you still cannot use them. Hence, you must win them over by treating them humanely and keep them in line with strict military discipline. This will ensure their allegiance.

If orders are consistently enforced in the training of soldiers, they will learn to obey; if orders are not enforced during training, they will not obey. When the authority of command is highly respected, then there is bound to be a harmonious relationship between the commander and his soldiers.

地形篇

【原文】

　　孙子曰：地形有通者，有挂者，有支者，有隘者，有险者，有远者。我可以往，彼可以来，曰通；通形者，先居高阳，利粮道，以战则利。可以往，难以返，曰挂；挂形者，敌无备，出而胜之；敌若有备，出而不胜，难以返，不利。我出而不利，彼出而不利，曰支；支形者，敌虽利

【今译】

　　孙子说：地形有"通形"、"挂形"、"支形"、"隘形"、"险形"、"远形"。我们可以去，敌人可以来的地域叫通形；在通形地域上，应先占领视界开阔的高地，保证粮道畅通，这样作战就有利。可以前往，难以返回的地域叫挂形；在挂形地域上，如果敌人没有防备，就可以突然出击而战胜它；如果敌人有防备，出击不能取胜，难以返回，就不利了。我军出击不利，敌人出击也不利的地域叫支形；在支形地域

86

The Terrain

Sunzi said:

There are the following six kinds of terrain: *tong* (通) — that which is accessible; *gua* (挂) — that which enmeshes; *zhi* (支) — that which is disadvantageous to both sides; *ai* (隘) — that which is narrow and precipitous; *xian* (险) — that which is hazardous; and *yuan* (远) — that which is distant.

Terrain which both armies can approach freely is called *tong*. On such a terrain, he who first occupies the sunny high ground and establishes convenient supply routes has the advantage in battle.

Terrain which allows entry but is hard to leave is called *gua*. The nature of this terrain is such that if the enemy is unprepared and you go out to engage him, you might defeat him. But when the enemy is prepared and you go out to engage him, you will not only fail to defeat him, but will have difficulty getting out. Consequently, you will be in trouble.

Terrain equally disadvantageous for either side to enter is called *zhi*. On this kind of terrain,

【原文】

我,我无出也;引而去之,令敌半出而击之,利。隘形者,我先居之,必盈之以待敌;若敌先居之,盈而勿从,不盈而从之。险形者,我先居之,必居高阳以待敌;若敌先居之,引而去之,勿从也。远形者,势均,难以挑战,战而不利。凡此六者,地之道也;将之至任,不可不察也。

【今译】

上,敌人虽然以利诱我,也不要出击,而应引兵离去,当敌人前出一半时再回兵攻击,这样就有利。在隘形地域上,我军应先敌占领,并封锁隘口等待敌人;如果敌人先占领隘口,并用重兵据守,就不要去打。如果没有封锁隘口,则可以去打。在险形地域上,如果我军先敌占领,必须控制视界开阔的高地,以等待来犯之敌;如果敌人先占领,就应引兵离去,不要去打它。在远形地域上,双方势均力敌,不宜挑战,勉强求战,则不利。以上六条,是利用地形的原则;是将帅的重大责任,不可不认真考察研究。

even if the enemy tempts you, you must not take the bait, but should withdraw. Having lured the enemy halfway out, you can then strike to your advantage.

On *ai* terrain, if you can occupy the pass first, you must fully garrison it and await the enemy approach. Should the enemy occupy and garrison such a pass first, you should not seek battle. But if he fails to garrison it, you may launch an attack.

As to *xian* terrain, if you occupy it first, you must take the high ground on the sunny side and await the enemy. In case the enemy occupies it first, you must quit the place and refrain from pursuing him. And in the case of *yuan*, that is when the enemy is some distance away, if both sides are evenly matched in strength, it is not easy to provoke a battle, and taking the battle to the enemy is not to your advantage.

Now these are the six rules governing the use of terrain. It is the commander's responsibility to study them with the utmost care.

【原文】

故兵有走者,有弛者,有陷者,有崩者,有乱者,有北者。凡此六者,非天之灾,将之过也。夫势均,以一击十,曰走。卒强吏弱,曰弛。吏强卒弱,曰陷。大吏怒而不服,遇敌怼而自战,将不知其能,曰崩。将弱不严,教道不明,吏卒无常,陈兵纵横,曰乱。将不能料敌,以少合众,以弱击强,兵无选锋,曰北。凡此六者,败之道也;将之至任,不可不察也。

【今译】

军事上有"走"、"弛"、"陷"、"崩"、"乱"、"北"六种情况。这六种情况,不是天灾造成的,而是将帅的过错造成的。凡是势均力敌而以一击十的,叫做"走"。兵卒强干,军官软弱的,叫做"弛"。军官强干,兵卒懦弱的,叫做"陷"。高级军吏愤怒而不服从指挥,遇到敌人怨忿而擅自出战,将帅又不了解他们的能力的,叫做"崩"。将帅懦弱不严、治军无方,军吏士卒不受军纪约束,出兵列阵杂乱无章的,叫做"乱"。将帅不能正确判断敌情,以少击众,以弱击强,军队又没有"选锋"的,叫做"北"。以上六种情况,都是造成失败的原因;是将帅的重大责任,不可不认真考察研究。

In warfare, there are six calamitous situations, namely, flight, insubordination, deterioration, ruin, chaos and rout. These are not caused by nature; rather they are the fault of the commander.

When the strategic advantages of the two sides are about the same, for an army to attack an enemy ten times its size will result in flight. If the soldiers are strong but the officers weak, the result will be insubordination. If the officers are strong but the soldiers weak, the result will be deterioration. If a frontline officer gets into a rage and becomes insubordinate and, on encountering the enemy, allows his resentment to spur him into unauthorized engagements, and the commander has no idea of that officer's capabilities, the result will be ruin. If the commander is weak and incompetent and his leadership lax, if there are no consistent rules to guide the officers and men and if his military formations are in disarray, the result will be chaos. If the commander, unable to assess his enemy, sends a small force to engage a large one, pits his weak forces against the enemy's strong, and operates without a vanguard of crack troops, the result will be rout. These are the six ways to certain defeat. It is the responsibility of the commander to examine them thoroughly.

【原文】

夫地形者,兵之助也。料敌制胜,计险阨远近,上将之道也。知此而用战者必胜,不知此而用战者必败。

故战道必胜,主曰无战,必战可也;战道不胜,主曰必战,无战可也。故进不求名,退不避罪,唯人是保,而利合于主,国之宝也。

视卒如婴儿,故可与之赴深溪;视卒如爱

【今译】

地形是用兵的辅助条件。判断敌情,夺取胜利,考察地形的险隘和道路的远近,这是高明的将领必须掌握的方法。懂得这些道理去指挥作战的,必然胜利;不懂得这些道理去指挥作战的,必然失败。

从战争规律上分析,必然会胜利的,即使国君说不打,也可以坚持打;从战争规律上分析,不能打胜的,即使国君说一定要打,也可以不去打。进不求名利,退不避罪责,只求保全民众而有利于国君,这样的将帅,才是国家的珍宝。

对待兵卒如同对待婴儿,兵卒就能与他共赴危难;对待兵卒如同对待爱子,兵卒就能

Advantageous terrain can be a natural ally in battle. Superior military leadership lies in the ability to assess the enemy's situation and create conditions for victory, to analyze natural hazards and calculate distances. He who fights with full knowledge of these factors is certain to win; he who fights without this knowledge is certain to lose.

Thus, if the way of war guarantees you victory, it is right for you to insist on fighting even if the sovereign has said not to. Where the way of war does not allow victory, it is right for you to refuse to fight even if the sovereign says you must. Therefore, a commander who decides to advance without any thought of winning personal fame and to withdraw without fear of punishment and whose only concern is to protect his people and serve his sovereign is an invaluable asset to the state.

Because he cares for his soldiers as if they were infants, they will follow him through the greatest dangers. Because he loves his soldiers

【原文】

子,故可与之俱死。厚而不能使,爱而不能令,乱而不能治,譬若骄子,不可用也。

知吾卒之可以击,而不知敌之不可击,胜之半也;知敌之可击,而不知吾卒之不可以击,胜之半也;知敌之可击,知吾卒之可以击,而不知地形之不可以战,胜之半也。

故知兵者,动而不迷,举而不穷。故曰:知彼知己,胜乃不殆;知天知地,胜乃不穷。

【今译】

与他同生共死。对待兵卒厚养而不使用,爱宠而不教育,违法而不惩治,那就好比受溺爱的骄子,是不能用来打仗的。

只了解自己的部队能打,而不了解敌人不可以打,胜利的可能只有一半;了解敌人可以打,而不了解自己的部队不能打,胜利的可能只有一半;了解敌人可以打,也了解自己的部队能打,而不了解地形不利于打,胜利的可能也只有一半。

所以,懂得用兵的人,他行动起来决不迷惑,他的对敌之策变化无穷。所以说:了解对方,了解自己,争取胜利就不会有危险;懂得天时,懂得地利,胜利就可保万全。

as if they were his own sons, they will stand by him even unto death. However, if the commander indulges his troops to the point he cannot use them, if he dotes on them to the point he cannot enforce his orders, if his troops are disorderly and he is unable to control them, they will be like spoiled children and useless.

To know that your troops are capable of striking at the enemy but not to know that he is invulnerable to attack reduces your chances of victory to half. To know that the enemy is vulnerable to attack but not to know that your troops are incapable of striking at him again reduces to half your chances of victory. To know that the enemy is vulnerable to attack and that your troops are capable of attacking, but not to know that the terrain does not favor you in battle once again reduces your chances of victory to half.

So it is that those who are well versed in warfare are never bewildered when they take action and their resourcefulness in overcoming the enemy is limitless.

Therefore, it is said: Know your enemy and know yourself, victory will not be at risk; know both heaven and earth, and victory will be complete.

九地篇

【原文】

孙子曰:用兵之法,有散地,有轻地,有争
地,有交地,有衢地,有重地,有圮地,有围地,
有死地。诸侯自战其地,为散地。入人之地
而不深者,为轻地。我得则利,彼得亦利者,
为争地。我可以往,彼可以来者,为交地。
诸侯之地三属,先至而得天下之众者,为衢地。

【今译】

孙子说:按照用兵的法则,有散地、有轻
地、有争地、有交地、有衢地、有重地、有圮地、
有围地、有死地。诸侯在本国境内作战的地
区,是散地。进入敌国浅近作战的地区,是轻
地。我军得到有利,敌军得到也有利的地区,
是争地。我军可以往,敌军可以来的地区,是
交地。三国交界、先到就可以得到诸侯列国
援助的地区,是衢地。深入敌境、远离城邑的

Nine Regions

Sunzi said:

In the art of employing troops, there are nine kinds of regions to consider: dispersive (*san* 散), marginal (*qing* 轻), contested (*zheng* 争), open (*jiao* 交), focal (*qu* 衢), critical (*zhong* 重), difficult (*pi* 圮), beleaguered (*wei* 围) and deadly (*si* 死). When the battle is fought within the territory of one's own state, it is a region that makes for the dispersion of his troops. Where one has penetrated into enemy territory only for a short distance, it constitutes a marginal region. A region that can give whoever occupies it first an advantage is a contested one. A region accessible to both sides is an open region. Territory where the borders of several neighbouring states meet is a focal region. The first to reach it will gain the allegi-

【原文】

入人之地深,背城邑多者,为重地。行山林、险阻、沮泽,凡难行之道者,为圮地。所由入者隘,所从归者迂,彼寡可以击吾之众者,为围地。疾战则存,不疾战则亡者,为死地。

是故散地则无战,轻地则无止,争地则无攻,交地则无绝,衢地则合交,重地则掠,圮地则行,围地则谋,死地则战。

所谓古之善用兵者,能使敌人前后不相

【今译】

地区,是重地。行于山林、险阻、沼泽,凡是难于通行的地区,是圮地。进入的道路狭隘、退归的道路迂远、敌军能够以其少击我之多的地区,是围地。迅速奋勇作战就能生存、不迅速奋勇作战就只有死亡的地区,是死地。

因此,散地,不宜作战;轻地,不宜停留;争地,不要在被动情况下进攻;交地,部队的联系不可断绝;衢地,则应结交诸侯;重地,就要掠取;圮地,就要迅速通过;围地,就要运谋设计;死地,就要奋勇作战、死里求生。

所谓古代善于指挥作战的人,能使敌人的部队前后不相策应,主力和小部队不相依

ance of the other states. When an army has penetrated deep into enemy territory and has left many cities behind, it is in a critical region. Mountains and forests, passes and natural hazards, wetlands and marshes and roads difficult to traverse constitute a difficult region. Where the road of entry is narrow and that of exit tortuous and where it can be guarded easily by just a small force, it is a beleaguered region. Ground on which you will survive only if you fight with all your might and will perish if you fail to do so is a deadly region.

That being the case, do not fight in a dispersive region; do not linger in a marginal region; do not strain to attack the enemy in a contested region; do not get cut off in an open region; form alliances with neighboring states in a focal region; plunder the enemy's resources in a critical region, press ahead in a difficult region; devise contingency plans in a beleaguered region; and summon up all your courage and energy to fight in a deadly region.

In ancient times, those described as skilled in war were able to reduce the enemy to such a state that his vanguard and rearguard could not

【原文】

及,众寡不相恃,贵贱不相救,上下不相收,卒离而不集,兵合而不齐。合于利而动,不合于利而止。

敢问:"敌众整而将来,待之若何?"曰:"先夺其所爱,则听矣。"兵之情主速,乘人之不及,由不虞之道,攻其所不戒也。

凡为客之道,深入则专,主人不克;掠于饶野,三军足食;谨养而勿劳,并气积力;运兵

【今译】

靠,官兵不相援救,上下不能协调,兵卒溃散难以集中,与敌交战阵形也不整齐。合于利就行动,不合于利就停止。

请问:"假如敌军人数众多、阵势严整地向我进发,用什么办法对付它呢?"回答是:"先夺取敌人的要害,就能使它听从我的摆布了。"用兵之理贵在神速,乘敌人措手不及的时机,走敌人意料不到的道路,攻击敌人没有戒备的地方。

大凡对敌国进攻作战,其规律是,越深入敌境,军心士气越专一,敌人越不能取胜。掠取粮草于丰饶的田野,全军就能得到足够的粮食;休整部队不使疲劳,提高士气积蓄力

be of help to each other, that his main force and his special detachments could not support each other, that his officers and men could not come to each other's aid, that the superiors and sub-ordinates could not coordinate their actions and that his forces were scattered and could not re-group, and even when they assembled, they could not form ranks.

If it was to the advantage of these skilful com-manders, they would move into action; if not, they would refrain from taking action. To the question, "What shall we do if a large and well-organized army marches against us?" the answer is: "Seize whatever the enemy prizes most and he will do what you wish him to do." In war, speed is the overriding consideration. This means: Catch the enemy unawares, make your way by unexpected routes and attack where he is least prepared.

For an invading army, the general rule of op-eration is: The deeper you penetrate into enemy territory, the greater the cohesion of your troops, and the less likely the host army will prevail over you. Plunder the enemy's most fer-tile fields, and your army will have ample provi-sions. Do not let your forces get worn down, boost their morale and conserve their strength. Deploy your troops and plan your strategies

【原文】

计谋,为不可测。投之无所往,死且不北,死焉不得,士人尽力。兵士甚陷则不惧,无所往则固,深入则拘,不得已则斗。是故其兵不修而戒,不求而得,不约而亲,不令而信。禁祥去疑,至死无所之。吾士无余财,非恶货也;无余命,非恶寿也。令发之日,士卒坐者涕沾襟,偃卧者涕交颐。投之无所往者,诸刿之勇也。

【今译】

量;部署兵力巧设计谋,使敌人无法判断我军意图。置部队于无路可走的境地,虽死也不会败退。既然死都不怕,官兵就都能尽力而战了。士卒深陷危险的境地就不恐惧,无路可走军心就会稳固,深入敌国军队就团结,迫不得已就坚决战斗。因此,这种条件下的军队,不须整饬就能注意戒备,不须强求就能完成任务,不须约束就能亲附拥戴,不须申令就能遵守纪律。禁止迷信消除疑虑,至死也不会逃避。我军士兵没有多余的钱财,不是厌恶财物;没有人贪生怕死,不是厌恶长寿。作战命令发布的时候,士兵们坐着的泪湿衣襟,躺着的泪流满面。把他们投入无路可走的绝地,就会像专诸、曹刿一样勇敢。

in such a way that the enemy cannot fathom your movements. Throw your troops into a situation from which there is no way out, and they will choose death over retreat. When your officers and men are ready to die, you will get nothing less than total exertion from them. Even when your troops are in the direst straits, they will not be afraid. With nowhere to turn, they will stand firm; having penetrated deep into enemy territory they will be united as one and, if need be, they will fight desperately and resolutely. Hence, an army under such conditions will be vigilant without admonishment, will carry out their duties without compulsion, will be devoted without constraint, will observe discipline even though they are not under close surveillance. Proscribe talk of omens and free the troops from apprehensions and they will not desert their units even till death.

Your officers do not have a surfeit of wealth, but it is not because they detest worldly goods; they are not afraid of death, but it is not because they detest longevity. Upon being ordered into action, tears may soak the garments of those sitting and wet the faces of those lying down. Yet when they are thrown into a situation where there is no way out, they will be as courageous as Zhuan Zhu, Cao Gui and other heroes of ancient times.

【原文】

故善用兵者,譬如率然;率然者,常山之蛇也。击其首则尾至,击其尾则首至,击其中则首尾俱至。敢问:"兵可使如率然乎?"曰:"可。"夫吴人与越人相恶也,当其同舟而济,遇风,其相救也如左右手。是故方马埋轮,未足恃也;齐勇若一,政之道也;刚柔皆得,地之理也。故善用兵者,携手若使一人,不得已也。

【今译】

善于统率部队的人,能使部队像"率然"一样。"率然"是常山的一种蛇。打它的头,尾巴就过来救应;打它的尾,头就过来救应;打它的身子,头尾都过来救应。试问:"可以使军队如同'率然'一样吗?"回答是:"可以。"吴国人和越国人是互相仇恨的,他们同船渡河,遇到大风,互相救援就像一个人的左右手。因此,缚住战马、掩埋车轮,是靠不住的。使部队上下齐力勇敢如一人,这是管理的方法问题;使强者弱者都能发挥作用,这是利用地形的法则问题。所以,善于用兵的人,能使全军携手如同一人,这是因为形势迫使它不得不这样。

Therefore, those who are skilled in employing troops are like the snake found on Mount Chang. If you strike its head, its tail will come to help; if you strike at its tail, its head will come to help; and if you strike at its middle, both head and tail will come to the rescue. Asked if an army can be trained to behave like the snake of Mount Chang, I say: Yes, it can. The people of Wu and the people of Yue hate each other. Yet if they were to cross the river in the same boat and were caught in a storm, they would come to each other's assistance as the right hand helps the left. Thus, it is not enough to tether the horses and bury the chariot wheels (tr.: *indicating determination to fight to the end*). The way of managing an army is to try to make the strong and the weak achieve a uniform level of courage, just as the proper utilization of terrain lies in making the best use of both the high and the lowlying grounds. The skilful commander can then lead his legions as though they were a single person who cannot but follow him.

【原文】

将军之事，静以幽，正以治。能愚士卒之耳目，使之无知。易其事，革其谋，使人无识；易其居，迂其途，使人不得虑。帅与之期，如登高而去其梯。帅与之深入诸侯之地，而发其机，焚舟破釜，若驱群羊，驱而往，驱而来，莫知所之。聚三军之众，投之于险，此谓将军之事也。九地之变，屈伸之利，人情之理，不可不察。

【今译】

统率部队这件事情，要冷静而幽邃，公正而严明。要能蒙蔽士卒的视听，使他们对军事行动毫无所知。变更作战部署，改变原定计划，使人们无法识破；改换驻地，迂回前进，使人们推测不出意图。主帅与部属约期出战，如同登高而抽去梯子一样不能后退。主帅与部属深入诸侯国内，如同击发弩机射出的箭矢一样一往无前。烧掉船只，砸毁军锅，对待士卒如同驱赶羊群，赶过去，赶过来，他们不知要到哪里去。聚集全军，把他们投入危险的境地，这就是统率军队的要务。九种地形的不同处置，攻防进退的利害得失，官兵的不同心理，这些都不能不认真研究考察。

It is the responsibility of the commander to be calm and inscrutable, to be impartial and strict in enforcing discipline. To keep his officers and men ignorant of his battle plans, he must be able to "stop their ears and blind their eyes." He alters his arrangements and changes his plans to hide his intentions. He shifts his camp and takes circuitous routes to keep people from anticipating his moves. On the day he leads his troops into battle, it is like climbing up a high wall and kicking away the ladder behind him so that there is no retreat. He leads his troops deep into the territory of the neighbouring states, like an arrow released from the bow, flying straight ahead. When he wants to make a determined drive, he burns his boats and smashes his cooking pots. Like a shepherd driving his flock of sheep, he leads his men here and there with no one knowing where they are heading. He assembles his armies and plunges them into the depth of danger. These then are the concerns of a commander: The different handling of the nine kinds of regions, the advantages and disadvantages of being on the offensive or on the defensive and the vagaries of human nature — they must all be thoroughly looked into.

【原文】

　　凡为客之道,深则专,浅则散。去国越境而师者,绝地也;四达者,衢地也;入深者,重地也;入浅者,轻地也;背固前隘者,围地也;无所往者,死地也。是故散地,吾将一其志;轻地,吾将使之属;争地,吾将趋其后;

　　交地,吾将谨其守;衢地,吾将固其结;重地,吾将继其食;圮地,吾将进其涂;围地,吾将塞其阙;死地,吾将示之以不活。故兵之

【今译】

　　进攻敌国作战的规律是:进入敌国愈深,军心就愈稳定专一;进入愈浅,军心就愈容易涣散。离开本国进入敌国作战的地区,是绝地;四通八达的地区,是衢地;进入敌国纵深的地区,是重地;进入敌国浅近的地区,是轻地;背靠险固前临隘路的地区,是围地;无路可走的地区,是死地。所以,散地,我就要统一官兵的意志;轻地,我就要使营阵紧密相连;争地,我就要迅速迂回到敌后;

　　交地,我就要谨慎防守;衢地,我就要巩固与邻国的交往;重地,我就要补充军粮;圮地,我就要迅速通过;围地,我就要堵塞缺口;死地,我就要显示死战的决心。所以,军事上

The general rule of operation for an invading force is that the deeper your penetration into enemy territory, the greater the cohesion of your troops; the shallower the penetration, the slacker and more dispersive your forces become. When you leave your own territory and lead your forces across the border, you have reached a point of no return. When you are in a region crisscrossed by roads, you are in a focal region. When you have penetrated deep into enemy territory, you are in a critical region. When you have penetrated for a short distance, you are in a marginal region. When you have your back to heavily secured ground and you face a narrow defile, you are in a beleaguered region. When you have no way to turn, you are in a deadly region.

Therefore, in a region where the troops are easily dispersed, I ensure the officers and men are of one mind; in a marginal region, I deploy the units so that they would be closely connected; in an open region, I quickly detour the units to the enemy's rear; in a contested region, I pay particular attention to defence; in a focal region, I make sure to cement my alliances with the neighbouring states; in a critical region, I try to increase the supply of provisions; in difficult region, I pass through quickly; in a beleaguered region, I plug all the loopholes in my formation; in a deadly region, I show the troops my re-

【原文】

情,围则御,不得已则斗,过则从。

是故不知诸侯之谋者,不能预交;不知山林、险阻、沮泽之形者,不能行军;不用乡导者,不能得地利。四五者,不知一,非霸王之兵也。夫霸王之兵,伐大国,则其众不得聚;威加于敌,则其交不得合。是故不争天下之交,不养天下之权,信己之私,威加于敌,故其城可拔,

【今译】

的情势就是:被包围就要抵抗,迫不得已就要拼死战斗,陷入危险的境地就会听从指挥。

不了解诸侯各国的战略动向,就不能与之结交;不熟悉山林、险阻、湖沼等地形,就不能行军;不使用向导,就不能得到地利。这几方面,有一方面不了解,就不是霸王的军队。凡是霸王的军队,进攻大国,就能使其军民来不及动员集中;威力施加于敌,就能使其无法同别国结交。所以,不必争着同天下诸侯结交,不必在诸侯国培植自己的权势,只要伸展自己的战略意图,威力施加于敌国,那么敌国的池就可以拔取,城国都就可以毁

solve to fight to the bitter end. The military situation calls for the soldier to resist when surrounded, to fight when there is no other alternative, and to obey order although in desperate plight.

Unless you know the strategic intention of the sovereigns of the neighboring states, you should not enter into alliances with them; unless you know the lay of the land — its mountains and forests, its passes and natural hazards, its wetlands and marshes, you should not deploy your army on it; unless you employ local guides, you cannot turn the regions to your advantage. It is not the army of a hegemonic leader that lacks knowledge of any of these points. When the army of a hegemonic leader attacks a large state, it does not allow its enemy the time to assemble his forces; when it brings its influence to bear, it prevents its enemy from forming alliances with other states. For this reason, you need not strive to form alliances with other states or foster your own forces within those states; when you pursue your own strategic intentions and bring your influences to bear on the enemy, you can take his cities and demolish his capital.

【原文】

其国可隳。施无法之赏,悬无政之令;犯三军之众,若使一人。犯之以事,勿告以言,犯之以利,勿告以害。投之亡地然后存,陷之死地然后生。夫众陷于害,然后能为胜败。故为兵之事,在于顺详敌之意,并敌一向,千里杀将,此谓巧能成事者也。

是故政举之日,夷关折符,无通其使,厉于廊庙之上,以诛其事。敌人开阖,必亟入之。先其

【今译】

灭。施行超越常规的奖赏;颁布打破常规的号令;指挥全军如同指挥一个人。给予任务,不说明企图,只告知有利条件,不说明危险因素。把士卒投入亡地才能转危为存,陷士卒于死地然后才能转死为生。军队陷入险境,然后才能夺取胜利。所以,指挥战争这件事,在于谨慎地观察敌人的战略意图,集中兵力于主攻方向,出兵千里斩杀其将,这就是所谓用巧妙的方法取得成功。

因此,决定作战行动之日,就要封锁关口销毁符证,禁止敌国使节往来,在庙堂秘密谋划,作出战略决策。敌方一旦出现间隙,就必

Confer extraordinary rewards and promulgate extraordinary regulations, and you can command the entire army as if it were one man. Assign the troops their tasks but do not reveal your plans, let them know the advantages but do not reveal the dangers. Only when you throw them into life-and-death situations will they fight to survive. Only when you plunge them into places where there is no way out will they fight to stay alive. Only when the rank and file find themselves in a perilous situation will they turn defeat into victory. Therefore, the concern of a commander lies in carefully studying the designs of the enemy and concentrating his forces on the main thrust; then he can slay the enemy commander 1,000 *li* away. Thus, by using his ingenuity and skill, he can work wonders.

For this reason, on the day the course of war is to be decided, close off the passes, destroy the official tallies and forbid the passage of enemy emissaries. Discuss the plans secretly and finalize your strategy in the ancestral temple. Once an opening appears in the enemy's de-

【原文】

所爱，微与之期。践墨随敌，以决战事。是故始如处女，敌人开户，后如脱兔，敌不及拒。

【今译】

须迅速乘机进入。首先夺取战略要地，但不要轻易约期决战。破除陈规，敌变我变，灵活决定自己的作战行动。因此，战争开始之前要像处女那样沉静，诱使敌人暴露弱点，战争展开之后要像脱逃的野兔一样迅速行动，使敌人来不及抵抗。

fense, you must grasp the opportunity and rush your troops in. Seize the strategic points first, but do not lightly agree to a date for the decisive battle. Be flexible when you decide your movements, ever ready to revise them according to the changing posture of the enemy. Thus, before action starts, appear as shy as a maiden and the enemy will relax his vigilance and leave his door open; once the fighting begins, move as swiftly as a scurrying rabbit and the enemy will find it is too late to put up a resistance.

火攻篇

孙子曰：凡火攻有五：一曰火人，二曰火积，三曰火辎，四曰火库，五曰火队。行火必有因，烟火必素具。发火有时，起火有日。时者，天之燥也；日者，月在箕、壁、翼、轸也，凡此四宿者，风起之日也。

孙子说：火攻有五种：一是火烧敌军人马，二是火烧敌军粮草，三是火烧敌军辎重，四是火烧敌军仓库，五是火烧敌军粮道。实施火攻必须有一定的条件，烟火器材必须素有准备。放火要看天时，点火要看日子。天时是指气候干燥，日子是指月亮行经箕、壁、翼、轸四星宿的位置时。月亮经过这四星宿时，正是有风的日子。

Attacking by Fire

Sunzi said:

There are five targets for an attack with fire: 1) men and horses, 2) grain and fodder, 3) wagons and equipment, 4) warehouses, and 5) supply routes. To launch a fire attack, certain conditions are required. Materials for setting the fire must always be on hand. There are appropriate weather and appropriate days to start a fire. Dry weather is the best for using fire attacks and the days when the moon passes through the constellations of the Winnowing Basket, the Wall, the Wings and the Chariot Platform are the best for launching a fire attack because those are generally the days when the winds rise.

【原文】

凡火攻,必因五火之变而应之。火发于内,则早应之于外。火发兵静者,待而勿攻,极其火力,可从而从之,不可从而止。火可发于外,无待于内,以时发之。火发上风,无攻下风。昼风久,夜风止。凡军必知有五火之变,以数守之。

故以火佐攻者明,以水佐攻者强。水可以绝,不可以夺。

【今译】

凡进行火攻,必须根据五种火攻方式的不同实施灵活地派兵配合。火从敌营内部放,就要及早派兵从外部策应;火已烧起而敌营毫无动静,则应冷静等待,不可立即发起进攻,待火势旺盛,可以进攻就进攻,不可进攻就停止。火也可以从外部放,这就不必等待内应,只要适时放火就行。火在上风放,不可从下风进攻。白天刮风的时间长,夜晚风就会停止。军队必须懂得灵活运用五种火攻形式,等待条件进行火攻。

用火来配合进攻效果显著,用水来配合进攻力量强大。水可以分割断绝敌军,但不能夺敌物资。

In attacking with fire, you must respond flexibly to changing conditions and deploy your troops accordingly: when a fire breaks out inside the enemy camp, respond at once with an attack from outside. If, in spite of the outbreak of fire, the enemy troops remain calm, bide your time and do not attack. Let the fire reach its height, then if you can follow through with an attack, do so; if not, stay where you are. If the fire is started from outside the enemy camp, do not wait for action from agents inside, just set the fire at the right time. If the fire is set upwind, do not attack from downwind. If the wind blows persistently during the day, it will probably die down at night. In all cases, the army must know which of the five kinds of fire attack to use according to the different situations and wait for the right time to strike.

Using fire to assist in attacks can produce notable results; using the method of inundation can make the attacks more powerful. However, while inundation can cut an enemy off, it cannot deprive him of his supplies and equipment.

【原文】

夫战胜攻取,而不修其攻者凶,命曰费留。故曰:明主虑之,良将修之。非利不动,非得不用,非危不战。主不可以怒而兴师,将不可以愠而致战。合于利而动,不合于利而止。怒可以复喜,愠可以复悦,亡国不可以复存,死者不可以复生。故明君慎之,良将警之,此安国全军之道也。

【今译】

凡打了胜仗、夺取了土地城邑,但不巩固战果的,则有凶险,这就叫做"费留"。所以说:明智的国君要慎重地考虑它,贤良的将帅要认真地处理它。不是有利不行动,不是能胜不用兵,不是危急不出战。国君不可因一时之怒而发动战争,将帅不可因一时之忿而出阵求战。有利才用兵,不利就停止。愤怒可以重新转为喜悦,气忿可以重新转为高兴,国家亡了就不能复存,人死了就不能再生。所以,明智的国君要慎重,贤良的将帅要警惕,这是安定国家、保全军队的关键。

To win battles and seize land and cities and yet fail to consolidate these achievements is fraught with dangers as it means a drain on your resources. Therefore it is said that a wise sovereign makes careful deliberations before launching a war and a good commander handles it with care. Do not go into battle if it is not in the interest of the state. Do not deploy the troops if you are not sure of victory. Do not send them into battle if you are not in danger. The sovereign should not start a war simply out of anger; the commander or general should not fight a battle simply because he is resentful. Take action only if it is to your advantage. Otherwise, do not. For an enraged man may regain his composure and a resentful person his happiness, but a state which has perished cannot be restored, nor can the dead be brought back to life.

Therefore, the enlightened sovereign approaches the question of war with utmost caution and the good commander warns himself against rash action. This is the way to keep the state secure and the army intact.

用间篇

【原文】

孙子曰:凡兴师十万,出征千里,百姓之费,公家之奉,日费千金;内外骚动,怠于道路,不得操事者,七十万家。相守数年,以争一日之胜,而爱爵禄百金,不知敌之情者,不仁之至也,非人之将也,非主之佐也,非胜之主也。故明君贤将,所以动而胜人,成功出于众者,先知

【今译】

孙子说:凡是兴兵十万,出征千里,百姓的耗费,公室的开支,每天要花费千金;国内外一片骚动,为运输物资而疲于道路、不能耕作的,有七十万家。相持数年,就是为了争取最后一天的胜利。吝惜爵禄金钱而不重用间谍,以致不了解敌情而致失败,那就是不仁到了极点,这种人不配称军队的统帅,不配作君主的助手,不配为胜利的主宰。贤明的君主、优秀的将帅之所以一出兵就能战胜敌人,成功超出众

Using Spies

Sunzi said:

Now, when an army of 100,000 is raised and sent on a distant campaign, the expenses borne by the people, together with the disbursements of the treasury, will amount to a thousand pieces of gold daily. There will be continuous commotion at home and abroad. As many as 700,000 households will be unable to pursue their farm work, exhausted as they are by their toil on the roads. The two armies may confront each other for years before the day comes for the decisive battle. Therefore, a commander shows extreme lack of consideration for his people if he is too stingy to grant ranks, honors and a hundred pieces of gold to his spies and, as a result, loses the battle because he is ignorant of the enemy's situation. Such a person is no commander worthy of his soldiers, no counselor worthy of his sovereign, no master of victory.

The enlightened sovereign and the capable commander conquer the enemy at every move and achieve successes far surpassing those of

【原文】

也。先知者,不可取于鬼神,不可象于事,不可验于度,必取于人,知敌之情者也。

故用间有五:有因间,有内间,有反间,有死间,有生间。五间俱起,莫知其道,是谓神纪,人君之宝也。因间者,因其乡人而用之。内间者,因其官人而用之。反间者,因其敌间而用之。死间者,为诳事于外,令吾间知之,而

【今译】

人之上,就在于事先了解敌情。事先了解敌情,不可祈求于鬼神,不可类比推测,不可用日月星辰运行的度数去验证,只能从人、从知道敌情的人的身上去了解。

使用间谍的方式有五种:有因间、内间、反间、死间、生间。五种间谍都使用起来,使敌人无从了解我用间的规律,这是神妙莫测之道,是国君的法宝。因间,是利用敌国的乡野之民充当间谍。内间,是利用敌方的官吏充当间谍。反间,是利用敌方间谍充当我方间谍。死间,就是将假情报传播于外,让潜入敌营的我

ordinary people because they possess "fore-knowledge". This "foreknowledge" cannot be obtained from ghosts or spirits, nor from gods, nor by analogy with past events, nor from astrological calculations. It can only come from men who know the enemy situation.

Hence the use of spies, of whom there are five kinds, namely, the native, the internal, the converted, the expendable and the surviving agents. When these five kinds of agents operate simultaneously and with total secrecy in their methods of operation, it can work miracles. This magical weapon constitutes a real treasure for the sovereign.

A native agent is the enemy's own countryman in your employ.

An internal agent is an enemy official whom you employ.

A converted agent, or double agent, is an enemy spy whom you employ.

An expendable agent is one who is deliberately given false information to mislead the enemy.

【原文】

传于敌间也。生间者,反报也。

故三军之事,莫亲于间,赏莫厚于间,事莫密于间。非圣智不能用间,非仁义不能使间,非微妙不能得间之实。微哉! 微哉! 无所不用间也。间事未发,而先闻者,间与所告者皆死。

凡军之所欲击,城之所欲攻,人之所欲杀,必先知其守将、左右、谒者、门者、舍人之

【今译】

方间谍得知,并传给敌间。生间,就是能活着回来报告情况的间谍。

所以在军队的关系中,没有比间谍更亲近的,奖赏没有比间谍更优厚的,事情没有比间谍更秘密的。不是圣贤睿智的人不能利用间谍,不是仁义的人不能指使间谍,不是用心微妙的人不能得到间谍的真实情报。微妙呀! 微妙呀! 无事不需使用间谍。间谍的工作尚未进行而事先走漏了消息,那么间谍和他所告诉的人都要处死。

凡是要攻打的敌方军队,要攻占的敌方城堡,要刺杀的敌方官员,必须先了解其守城将官、左右亲信、掌管传达通报的官员、守门

A surviving agent is one who returns with information from the enemy camp.

Of all those in the army close to the commander, none is more intimate than the agents; of all rewards, none more liberal than those given to agents; of all matters, none more confidential than those relating to secret operations. He who lacks wisdom cannot use agents; he who is not humane and generous cannot direct agents; he who is not sensitive and alert cannot get the truth out of them. So delicate and so secretive is espionage that there is nowhere you cannot put it to good use.

But if plans relating to secret operations are prematurely divulged, the agent and all those to whom he has leaked the secret should be put to death.

Generally, whether the object is to crush an army, to storm a city, or to assassinate an enemy official, it is always necessary to begin by finding out the identities of the garrison commander, his staff officers, retainers, gate-keep-

【原文】

姓名,令吾间必索知之。必索敌人之间来间我者,因而利之,导而舍之,故反间可得而用也。因是而知之,故乡间、内间可得而使也。因是而知之,故死间为诳事,可使告敌。因是而知之,故生间可使如期。五间之事,主必知之,知之必在于反间,故反间不可不厚也。

昔殷之兴也,伊挚在夏;周之兴也,吕牙

【今译】

官吏和近侍门人的姓名,命我方间谍务必侦察清楚。

必须搜索出前来侦察我军的敌方间谍,根据情况利用收买、诱导放归,这样反间就可以为我所用了。由此而了解情况,于是乡间、内间就可以为我所用了。由此而了解情况,于是就能使死间传假情报给敌人。由此而了解情况,于是就可以使生间按预定时间回报敌情。五种间谍的使用,国君都必须知道,了解情况的关键在于反间,所以对反间不可不厚待。

从前殷朝的兴起,是因为伊挚曾经在夏朝;周朝的兴起,是因为吕牙曾经在殷朝。所

ers and guards. The agents must be directed to obtain this information. It is essential to find out who the enemy agents are who have been sent to spy on you and to bribe them into serving you. Give them instructions and send them back home. This is how converted agents are recruited and used. It is through the information provided by the converted agents that native and internal agents are recruited and used, that the expendable agents can be sent to pass on false information to the enemy, and that the surviving agents can come back with the needed information as scheduled. The sovereign must be fully aware of the activities of all five kinds of agents. And it is the converted agent who is crucial to his obtaining the needed information. Therefore, he must treat the latter with the utmost generosity.

In ancient times, Yi Zhi, who had served the Xia Dynasty, was instrumental in the rise of the Yin (Shang) Dynasty over Xia. Likewise, Lu Ya, who had served the Yin Dynasty, had much to do with the rise of the succeeding Zhou Dynasty.

【原文】

在殷。故惟明君贤将，能以上智为间者，必成大功，此兵之要，三军之所恃而动也。

【今译】

以，贤明的国君、优秀的将帅，能用智谋超群的人为间谍，就一定能建树大功，这是用兵的关键，全军要依靠它来决定军事行动。

Therefore, only the enlightened sovereign and wise commander who are capable of using the most intelligent people as agents are destined to accomplish great things. Secret operations are essential in war; upon them the army relies in deciding its every move.

孙膑兵法

Sun Bin: The Art of War

擒庞涓

擒庞涓

　　昔者,梁君将攻邯郸,使将军庞涓、带甲八万至于茬丘。齐君闻之,使将军忌子、带甲八万至……竞。庞子攻卫□□□,将军忌〔子〕……□卫□□救与……救卫是失令"。田忌曰:"若不救卫,将何为?"孙子曰:"请南攻平陵。平陵其城小而县大,人众甲兵盛,东阳战

【今译】

　　从前,魏惠王准备攻取赵国的都城邯郸,派遣将军庞涓率领八万军队进驻茬丘。齐威王听到这个消息,也派将军田忌率领八万军队到达齐境。庞涓攻打卫国,将军田忌问道,……是否要救援卫国? 孙膑回答说:"救援卫国,是违反军令。"田忌又问道:"如果不救卫国,应该怎么办呢?"孙膑说:"请率军南下,攻打平陵。平陵这个地方,城虽小,县境却很

The Capture Of Pang Juan

Formerly, when King Hui of the State of Wei
(魏) wanted to attack Handan, capital of the
State of Zhao (赵), he sent General Pang Juan as
the head of an 80,000-strong army. This came to
the knowledge of King Wei (威) of the State of Qi
(齐). He therefore sent General Tian Ji with 80,
000 troops to his country's frontiers. When Pang
Juan attacked the State of Wei (卫), General Tian
asked... "Should we send our forces to help Wei
(卫)?" "To do so," answered Sun Bin, "would
go against the rules of warfare." "What else can
we do if we don't go and help them?" asked
Tian.

"I would suggest you move your forces to the
south and attack Pingling," Sun Bin answered.
"This is a county with a small town but a large
territory. It has a large population protected by a
strong army, and is a major military post in the

【原文】

邑,难攻也。吾将示之疑。吾攻平陵,南有宋,北有卫,当途有市丘,是吾粮途绝也。吾将示之不知事。"

于是徙舍而走平陵。〔□□〕陵,忌子召孙子而问曰:"事将何为?"孙子曰:"都大夫孰为不识事?"曰:"齐城、高唐。"孙子曰:"请取所□□□□□□□□□□二大夫□以□□□臧□都横卷四达环涂□横卷所□陈也。环涂铍甲之所处也。吾末甲

【今译】

大,人口众多,兵力强盛,是东部地区的军事重镇,很难攻取。我打算用假象欺骗敌人。我军攻打平陵,南面有宋国,北面有卫国,途中有市丘,这就使我军的运粮通道被断绝了。从而给敌人造成我们不懂得用兵的错觉。"

于是,齐军拔营,直趋平陵。快到平陵时,田忌召见孙膑问道:"仗应该如何打呢?"孙膑说:"我们的都邑大夫中有谁不懂得打仗的事?"田忌说:"齐城、高唐。"孙膑说:"请派齐城、高唐二位大夫去攻打平陵。……横、卷二邑四通八达,是魏国钻荼将军屯驻重兵、布阵设防的地

eastern region. It is very difficult to take. By assaulting it, I intend to mislead the enemy. When
we attack Pingling, our supply route will be in
danger because Pingling is hedged in by the State
of Song in the south and the State of Wei (卫) in
the north, with Shiqiu blocking our way. Thus,
we create the impression that we know nothing
about the art of war."

The Qi army then decamped and headed
straight for Pingling. As it approached the region,
General Tian asked Sun Bin, "How should we
fight this battle?" Sun Bin answered with a question, "Who among our city mayors know nothing
about the art of war?" Tian answered, "The mayors of Qizheng and Gaotang." "Please send them
to attack Pingling," Sun Bin suggested. He went
on to explain, "...The towns of Heng and Juan
have good road connections. They have a strong
defence, and are garrisoned by forces led by General Zuan Tu. Our follow-up troops are strong

【原文】

劲,本甲不断。环涂击柀其后,二大夫可杀也。"
于是段齐城、高唐为两,直将蚁傅平陵。挟菹环
涂夹击其后,齐城、高唐当术而大败。将军忌子
召孙子问曰:"吾攻平陵不得而亡齐城、高唐,当
术而蹶。事将何为?"孙子曰:"请遣轻车西驰梁
郊,以怒其气。分卒而从之,示之寡。"于是为
之。庞子果弃其辎重,兼取舍而至。孙子弗息
而击之桂陵,而擒庞涓。故曰,孙子之所以为者
尽矣。

四百六

【今译】

方。我军后续部队精锐,主力部队不分散。这
样,一旦钻荼切断齐城、高唐二位大夫的后路,
二位大夫可能牺牲。"于是,分齐城、高唐为两路
去直接攻打平陵。魏将挟菹、钻荼从侧后夹击,
齐城、高唐两路人马立即惨败。将军田忌召见
孙膑问道:"我军攻打平陵没有得手,齐城、高唐
两部当即惨败,仗该如何打呢?"孙膑回答说:
"请派遣战车迅速西进,直奔魏都大梁城郊,以
此激怒庞涓。同时分派士卒,纵使他们骂敌挑
战,以向敌人显示我军兵力单薄。"于是,按照孙
膑所说去办。庞涓果然丢弃辎重车辆,日夜兼
程回救大梁。孙膑在桂陵连续突击魏军,俘获
庞涓。

and our main forces are concentrated, but should Zuan Tu cut off the vanguard led by the mayors of Qicheng and Gaotang, they might have to pay with their lives. Tian therefore ordered the mayors of Qicheng and Gaotang to lead two detachments to assault Pingling, and of course they were roundly beaten by Wei generals Xia Die and Zuan Tu, who jointly launched a pincer attack from behind their flanks. General Tian again called in Sun Bin for consultation. "Our troops failed to take Pingling and both mayors suffered serious defeat. What shall we do next?" he asked. Sun Bin replied, "Please order your light chariots to move swiftly westward and head for the Wei (魏) capital of Daliang. This will provoke Pang Juan. At the same time, send some soldiers to insult the enemy. This will create the impression that we have an insufficient force."

General Tian did exactly what Sun Bin suggested. As a result, Pang Juan abandoned his heavy equipment and wagons and rushed back in an effort to save Daliang. At Guiling, the troops he led were intercepted and routed by Sun Bin's repeated attacks. Pang Juan was captured. Therefore, it is said that Sun Bin's tactics reached the peak of excellence.

〔见威王〕

【原文】

孙子见威王,曰:"夫兵者,非士恒势也。此先王之傅道也。战胜,则所以在亡国而继绝世也。战不胜,则所以削地而危社稷也。是故兵者不可不察。然夫乐兵者亡,而利胜者辱。兵

【今译】

孙膑见齐威王,说:"战争,不能倚恃某种固定不变的形势。这是先王传下来的道理。打了胜仗,就能保存处于危亡中的国家,继承濒于断绝的世系。打了败仗,就会使领土被削割、国家遭危害。因此,对战争问题不能不认真研究。好战的人会导致亡国,贪胜的人会导致屈辱。

140

An Audience with
King Wei

During an audience with King Wei (of the State of Qi), Sun Bin said:

"One has to take changing conditions into consideration when waging war. This is a principle our forebears have passed down to us. Victory in war will save an embattled country and its lineage will continue, whereas defeat will mean the loss of territory and the country's very existence will be jeopardized. Therefore, war is an issue that calls for careful study."

"Those who love war will lead the country to destruction and those who crave victory will

【原文】

非所乐也,而胜非所利也。事备而后动,故城小而守固者,有委也;卒寡而兵强者,有义也。夫守而无委,战而无义,天下无能以固且强者。尧有天下之时,黜王命而弗行者七,夷有二,中国四。故尧伐负海之国而后北方民得不苛,伐共工而后兵寝而不起,

【今译】

战争不是人们所喜爱的,胜利不是人们所贪求的。胜利条件具备了,然后才能行动。城小而防守坚固,是因为有充足的物资储备;兵少而战斗力很强,是因为正义在自己一方。防守而无物资储备,发动战争而不正义,天下谁也无法使其防守坚固、战斗力强大。唐尧治理天下时,废弃王命而拒不执行命令的有七个部落,东夷地区有两个,中原地区有四个。唐尧征伐靠海远方各国,从而使北方民众不受袭扰;讨伐共工,从而使战争消弭、

bring it dishonor. Therefore, war is not to be loved and the glory of victory not to be hankered after. Take action only when the conditions for victory are ripe. Some cities are small but have a strong defense because they are amply provisioned. Some armies are relatively small but are combat effective because justice is on their side. No one in the world can make a city impregnable if it is not properly provisioned. No one can make an army fight effective if it is fighting an unjust war. When Yao reigned, seven tribes refused to obey his orders. Two of these tribes were from the eastern region and four from the Central Plains. Yao mounted an expedition against the tribes by the sea and thus brought peace to the northern people. He launched an attack against Gong Gong (*tr.: said to be one of Yao's ministers*), putting an end to the continuous war with the result that the army was left with nothing to do.

【原文】

弛而不用。其间数年,尧身衰而治屈,胥天下而传舜。舜击灌兜,放之崇;击鲧,放之羽;击三苗,放之危;亡有扈氏中国。有苗民存,独为弘。舜身衰而治屈,胥天下而传之禹。禹凿孟门而通大夏,斩八林而焚九□。西面而并三苗□□……素佚而致利也。战胜而强立,故天下服矣。昔者,神农战斧遂;黄帝战蜀禄;尧伐共工;舜伐厥

【今译】

军队废止不用。数年之间,唐尧衰老治国无力,于是把天下传给虞舜。虞舜进攻灌兜,把他放逐到崇山;进攻鲧,把他放逐到羽山;进攻三苗,把他放逐到三危;后又灭掉了中原的有扈氏。有些三苗部族,则独自强大起来。虞舜衰老治国无力,于是把天下传给夏禹。夏禹开凿孟门,通达夏虚,砍伐许多森林,焚烧很多草木。向西翦除三苗……可见,(不能)无所作为而获得胜利。战胜敌人、强大巩固,天下都服从。从前,神农战补遂;黄帝战胜蚩尤于涿鹿;唐尧

Before long, Yao declined in years, and, becoming unfit to rule, passed on his reign to Shun. Shun defeated Huan Duo (*tr.: a tribal leader*) and exiled him to Chongshan. Likewise, he defeated Gun (*tr.: another tribal leader*) and exiled him to Yushan. He routed the ancient tribe of San Miao and exiled its members to San Wei, and later finished off Youhushi in the Central Plains. However, the survivors of the San Miao tribe grew powerful and disobedient. When Shun too reached old age, he passed on his reign to Yu. Yu established the Xia Dynasty. He excavated an opening in the ridge of Meng Men to drain the floodwaters of Da Xia, felled many virgin forests and set fire to meadows of wild grass to open up land for farming. He fought and conquered the San Miaos to the west... Thus, victory does not come easily, and only when one has vanquished one's enemies and become consolidated will he have the respect of the world.

"History has recorded that Shen Nong fought the tribe of Fu Sui, the Yellow Emperor defeated tribal chief Chiyou in a battle at Zhuolu, Yao led an expedition against Gong Gong, Shun cam-

【原文】

管;汤放桀;武王伐纣;帝奄反,故周公浅之。故曰,德不若五帝,而能不及三王,智不若周公,曰我将欲积仁义,式礼乐,垂衣裳,以禁争夺。此尧舜非弗欲也。不可得,故举兵绳之。"

【今译】

讨伐共工;虞舜讨伐厥管;商汤放逐夏桀;周武王讨伐殷纣王;商奄叛乱,周公率兵去镇压。所以说,那些功德不如五帝、才能不如三王、智略不如周公的人,却说什么我要用积仁义、用礼乐来禁止战争。这种办法尧舜不是不想采用,而根本办不到,所以才用战争来解决它。"

paigned against Jue Guang (*tr.: probably a tribal chief*), King Tang of the Shang Dynasty exiled Jie (*tr.: the last king of the Xia Dynasty*), King Wu of Zhou led an expedition against Zhou (*tr.: the last king of Yin*) and the Duke of Zhou waged a campaign to suppress a revolt by the state of Shanyan.

"Therefore, when some wiseacres whose achievements and virtues cannot compare with those of the Five Emperors (*tr.: there are several versions as to whom they refer to, but most of them include the Yellow Emperor, Yao and Shun*), whose talents cannot compare with those of the three Kings (*tr.: Yu, Tang and King Wen, each of whom started a dynasty*) and whose wisdom cannot compare with that of the Duke of Zhou, when they claim that they can end all conflicts and wars through benevolence, justice, modesty and rites, we say to them: Though both Yao and Shun would have preferred to have it that way, it was simply not feasible. That is why they resorted to war."

威王问

【原文】

威王问

　　齐威王问用兵孙子,曰:"两军相当,两将相望,皆坚而固,莫敢先举,为之奈何?"孙子答曰:"以轻卒尝之,贱而勇者将之,期于北,毋期于得,为之微阵以触其侧。是谓大得。"威王曰:"用众用寡有道乎?"孙子曰:"有。"威王曰:"我强敌弱,我众敌

【今译】

　　齐威王向孙膑询问用兵的方法,说:"两军旗鼓相当,双方将士互相对峙,阵势都很坚固,谁也不率先出击,应该怎么办呢?"孙膑回答说:"用轻装部队去试攻敌阵,由地位低下而又勇敢的人率领,务必打败仗,不准打胜仗,再用小部队去袭击敌军的翼侧。这是取得重大胜利的方法。"威王问:"使用较多的兵力和使用较小的兵力,在指挥作战上有规律吗?"孙膑说:"有。"威王问:"我强敌弱,我众敌

King Wei's Inquiries

King Wei consulted Sun Bin about the art of war.

"Given that the opposing sides are equal in strength and their troops face each other in a stalemate with neither side attacking first, what should we do?" he asked.

Sun Bin answered, "Probe the enemy's position with a light force led by a low-ranking officer who is courageous. His duty is not to win the battle but to suffer a small defeat. After that, send another small detachment to attack the enemy's flanks. This is the method you use to win a major victory."

The king continued his questioning. "Is there a difference in method between commanding a big force and a small force?" With a bow Sun Bin said there was. "What should we do when we are strong and numerous while the enemy is weak

【原文】

寡,用之奈何?"孙子再拜曰:"明王之问。夫众且强,犹问用之,则安国之道也。命之曰赞师。毁卒乱行,以顺其志,则必战矣。"威王曰:"敌众我寡,敌强我弱,用之奈何?"孙子曰:"命曰让威。必臧其尾,令之能归。长兵在前,短兵在□,为之流弩,以助其急者。□□毋动,以待敌能。"威王曰:"我出敌出,未知众少,用之奈何?"孙子〔曰〕:"命曰险成。

【今译】

寡,应该如何指挥呢?"孙膑再一次向威王行礼说:"这是圣君提出的问题。军队众多而又强大,还要问如何指挥,这是使国家安全的作法。在这种情况下指挥作战的方法叫'赞师'。就是故意使我军序列混乱、阵势不整,以便迎合敌人的心意,敌人就必然出战。"威王问:"敌众我寡,敌强我弱,应该怎样指挥呢?"孙膑答道:"这叫做'让威',即必须隐蔽好后面的主力部队,使他们能随时撤退。把长兵器配置在前列,把短兵器配置在后列,并配置一部分机动的弩兵,以便应付紧急情况。……不要轻易行动,以等待敌人暴露其真实的作战能力。"威王问:"我军开进,敌军也开进,双方遭遇,不知敌人兵力多少,应该如何指挥呢?"孙膑答道:"这叫做'险

and sparse?" Sun Bin, bowing again, replied, "That is the type of question a wise sovereign would ask. When your army is strong and numerous, and you still want to know how to direct your army, then you have the way to the security of the state. The method you should use in such a situation is called *zanshi*; that is, you must mislead the enemy into attacking you by setting up a seemingly helter-skelter formation to create the impression of confusion in your own ranks."

King Wei asked, "What if the enemy is strong and numerous and we are weak and few? Sun Bin said, "In that case, use the method known as *rangwei*, i.e., hide your main force in the back so that it can withdraw at any time necessary. The troops using long-armed weapons should be deployed in front, followed by troops using short-armed weapons and groups of mobile archers ready to meet any emergency... Do not rush into action. Wait for the enemy to reveal where his true strength lies."

"What should we do when we and our enemy are marching into the same area and have an encounter while we have no idea how strong the enemy is?" "This is a situation known as *xian-*

【原文】

险成,敌将为正,出为三阵,一□〔□□□〕能相助,可以止而止,可以行而行,毋求……"威王曰:"击穷寇奈何?"孙子"……可以待生计矣。"威王曰:"击均奈何?"孙子曰:"营而离之,我并卒而击之,毋令敌知之。然而不离,案而止。毋击疑。"威王曰:"以一击十,有道乎?"孙子曰:"有。攻其无备,出其不意。"威王曰:"地平卒齐,合而北者,何也?"孙子曰:

【今译】

成'。'险成',就是当敌人采用常规战法时,一般部署为三阵,……可驻扎就驻扎,可开进就开进,……"威王问:"攻击走投无路的穷寇应该怎么打呢?"孙膑回答道:"使敌人认为有生路可以等待。"威王问:"攻击势均力敌的敌军怎么打呢?"孙膑回答说:"迷惑敌人,分其兵力,我军集中兵力攻击它,不让敌人知道我军的意图。如果敌人不分散兵力,我军就按兵不动。不要去攻击情况不明的敌人。"威王问:"以一击十有什么办法吗?"孙膑答说:"有。这就是要攻其无备,出其不意。"威王问:"地形平坦,部伍严整,却失败了,是什么原因呢?"孙膑

cheng, and in such a situation, if the enemy uses a *zheng* tactic, you should generally deploy your troops in three formations... and they should advance or encamp as the circumstances require."

The king continued with his questions. "What should we do when the enemy finds himself in a perilous situation?" Sun Bin replied, "Make him believe that he still has a way out and can wait. The king asked, "And what if the enemy and we are evenly matched in strength?" "Confuse the enemy and make him disperse his forces while you concentrate your own to attack him. Do not reveal your intentions to the enemy. If the enemy refuses to disperse, then do not go into battle. Be sure not to attack an enemy whose strength and intentions you know nothing about."

The king asked, "Is there a way to attack an enemy ten times our strength?" "Yes, there is," answered Sun Bin, "and that is to attack when he is not expecting you and when he is unprepared." The king asked, "Why is it that sometimes when the terrain is favorable and the soldiers are orderly and yet the army fails in battle?"

【原文】

"其阵无锋也。"威王曰:"令民素听,奈何?"孙子曰:"素信。"威王曰:"善哉! 言兵势不穷。"

田忌问孙子曰:"患兵者何也? 困敌者何也? 壁延不得者何也? 失天者何也? 失地者何也? 失人者何也? 请问此六者有道乎?"孙子曰:"有。患兵者地也,困敌者险也。故曰,三里沮洳将患军……涉将留大甲。故曰,患

【今译】

说:"这是因为没有突破敌阵的先锋。"威王问:"要使士卒能够一贯听从命令,应该怎么办呢?"孙膑答道:"这就要一贯讲信用。"威王高兴地说:"真好啊! 你讲的用兵之道,确实奥妙无穷。"

田忌问孙膑说:"妨碍军队行动的是什么? 陷敌人于困境的是什么? 壁垒延道不能攻克的原因是什么? 不得天时的原因是什么? 不得地利的原因是什么? 不得人心的原因是什么? 请问处理这六个问题有什么规律吗?"孙膑说:"有。妨碍军队行动的是地形不利,陷敌于困境的是险阻要碍。所以说,周围有三里沼泽地,就会给军队的行动带来巨大的妨碍,……要通过沼泽泥泞地段或渡过江河,重装备就将被迫留下。因此说,妨碍军队

"It is because there is no spearhead to break through the enemy's ranks." "What should we do to make the soldiers observe discipline and always follow orders?" the king asked, to which Sun Bin replied, "Then you should always keep your word." The king expressed his pleasure with Sun Bin's answers, saying, "This is indeed excellent. There seem to be endless ways of conducting war."

Now it was Tian Ji's turn to ask questions.

"What is it that obstructs an army's advance? What is it that places the enemy in a quandary? Why is it that some ramparts and roads cannot be taken or overrun? Why is it that sometimes one fails to have heaven and earth on his side? And finally, why is it that one sometimes fails to gain the support of the people? Are there any rules in handling these matters?" he queried.

Sun Bin answered, "There are. It is unfavorable terrain which obstructs an army's advance. It is hazardous paths and major obstacles, which place the enemy in a quandary. That is why it is said that when an army is surrounded by three *li* of marshes, its advance is confronted with great difficulties. When passing through marshes or crossing rivers, the army has to leave behind its heavy equipment. Therefore, unfavorable terrain

【原文】

兵者地也,困敌者险也,壁延不得者蜚寒也,□……奈何?"孙子曰:"鼓而坐之,十而揄之。"田忌曰:"行阵已定,动而令士必听,奈何?"孙子曰:"严而示之利。"田忌曰:"赏罚者,兵之急者耶?"孙子曰:"非。夫赏者,所以喜众,令士忘死也。罚者,所以正乱,令民畏上也。可以益胜,非其急者也。"田忌曰:"权、

【今译】

行动的是地形不利,陷敌于困境的是险阻要碍,壁垒延道不能攻克的原因是因为建有渠幨设施,……"田忌问:"〔对此该〕怎么办?"孙膑说:"击鼓发出攻击令,但部队却坐阵待敌,同时用各种办法引诱、调动敌人。"田忌问:"阵已布好,交战时要使士卒能听从命令,怎么办?"孙膑说:"既要严明军纪,又要让士卒看到(立功受奖的)好处。"田忌问:"赏罚严明,是不是用兵最紧要的事情呢?"孙膑说:"不是。奖赏,是为了鼓舞士气,使士卒舍生忘死地战斗。惩罚,是为了整饬军纪,使士卒服从上级的指挥。这些都有助于胜利的取得,但不是用兵最紧要的事情。"田忌问:"权、

deters the army's march and places the enemy in a quandary. And the reason for not being able to take ramparts and roads is that they are provided with protective walls. . . ."

Tian Ji asked, "What then can I do?" Sun Bin answered, "Beat the drums to give the attack signal, but have the army stay put and wait for the enemy to attack. Meanwhile, try by all means to draw the enemy out."

Tian Ji asked, "When the formations have been laid out, what should I do so that the soldiers obey my orders?" Sun Bin answered, "You must enforce strict discipline while letting the soldiers see that whoever shows great merit will be rewarded." "Is the strict application of rewards and punishments the most crucial in commanding troops?" Tian Ji asked. "No," Sun Bin replied, "Rewards are given to boost morale so that the soldiers will be ready to give their lives to win the battle. Punishments are meted out to strengthen discipline so that the soldiers will obey their officers' orders. Both help to win victory but they are not the most crucial in waging war."

"Are authority, strategic advantage, strata-

【原文】

势、谋、诈,兵之急者耶?"孙子曰:"非也。夫权者,所以聚众也。势者,所以令士必斗也。谋者,所以令敌无备也。诈者,所以困敌也。可以益胜,非其急者也。"田忌忿然作色:"此六者皆善者所用,而子大夫曰非其急者也。然则其急者何也?"孙子曰:"料敌计险,必察远近,……将之道也。必攻不守,兵之急者也。□……骨也。"

【今译】

势、谋、诈,是不是用兵最紧要的事情呢?"孙膑说:"不是。掌握权力,是为了调集指挥军队。示形造势,是为了使士卒勇敢作战。运用计谋,是为了使敌人放松戒备。施展诡诈,是为了困惑敌人。这些都有助于胜利的取得,但不是用兵最紧要的事情。"田忌生气地说:"奖赏、惩罚、权力、形势、计谋、诡诈,这六个方面都是善于用兵的人所常用的,而您却说不是用兵最紧要的事情。那么用兵最紧要的事情是什么呢?"孙膑说:"分析敌人的情况,研究地形的险易,必须察明道路的远近,……这是将帅的重大责任。坚决打击敌人空虚而要害之处,这就是用兵最紧要的问题。……"

gem and deception the most crucial in waging war?" Tian Ji asked. "No," Sun Bin answered, "The purpose of having authority is to be able to assemble the troops; the purpose of gaining strategic advantage is to enable the soldiers to fight courageously in war; the purpose of using stratagem is to make the enemy relax his vigilance; and the purpose of using deception is to confuse the enemy. These can all help win victory for you, but they are not the most crucial in war."

Tian Ji became irritated and said, "Rewards and punishments, authority, strategic advantage, stratagem and deception — these are all widely used by capable commanders, and yet you say they are not the most crucial in waging war. Then tell me what is." Sun Bin continued with his dissertation. "Analyze the enemy's situation, study the intricacies of the terrain and check the distances... these are the major responsibilities of the commander.... The most crucial in waging war is to deal resolute blows at the enemy's

【原文】

田忌问孙子曰："张军毋战有道?"孙子曰："有。倅险增垒,诤戒毋动,毋可□前,毋可怒。"田忌曰:"敌众且武,必战有道乎?"孙子曰:"有。埤垒广志,严正辑众,避而骄之,引而劳之,攻其无备,出其不意,必以为久。"田忌问孙子曰:"锥行者何也? 雁行者何也? 选卒力士者何也?劲弩趋发者何也?飘风之阵者何也?众卒者何也?"孙子曰:"锥行者,

【今译】

田忌向孙膑问道:"摆开阵势而又不与敌交战,这有什么办法吗?"孙膑说:"有。据守险隘,增强壁垒,注意戒备,按兵不动,不脱离阵地,不为敌人激怒。"田忌问:"敌人既众多又凶猛,必须与它交战,有什么办法呢?"孙膑说:"有。增强壁垒,广泛动员,严明军令,整饬部队,团结士卒。避敌锐气使其骄傲,引诱调动敌人使其疲惫。然后攻其无备,出其不意。必须实行持久作战的方针。"田忌问孙膑道:"锥行阵的用处是什么? 雁行阵的用处是什么?选拔精锐士卒的作用是什么? 强弩劲射的作用是什么?飘风阵的作用是什么?普通士卒的作用是什么?"孙膑说:"锥行阵,用

vital and weak points...." Tian Ji then asked, "When the formations on both sides are pitted against each other but neither is ready to join battle, then what should I do?" Sun Bin answered, "What you should do is to guard the dangerous passes, strengthen the ramparts and keep your vigilance, but do not make the first move. Don't leave your position and don't be agitated by the enemy...."

Tian Ji asked, "When the enemy is numerous and ferocious, is there a way to take him on?" Sun Bin answered, "Yes, there is. Strengthen your bulwarks, mobilize your troops, enforce strict discipline, make the soldiers unite as one, avoid contact so as to make the enemy swollen-headed, entice the enemy so that he gets tired out and then attack him unexpectedly, catching him unprepared. Hence, it is necessary here to fight a protracted battle."

Tian Ji then asked Sun Bin about formations. "What are the functions of the cone and wild geese formations, crack contingents, powerful archery units, the wind formation and the rank-and-file troops?" Sun Bin answered: "The function

【原文】

所以冲坚毁锐也。雁行者,所以触侧应
□〔也〕。选卒力士者,所以绝阵取将也。劲弩
趋发者,所以甘战持久也。飘风之阵者,所以
回□〔□□也〕。众卒者,所以分功有胜也。"孙
子曰:"明主、知道之将,不以众卒几功。"
孙子出而弟子问曰:"威王、田忌,臣主之
问何如?"孙子曰:"威王问九,田忌问七,几知

【今译】

来破敌坚阵、歼敌锐卒。雁行阵,用来夹击敌
人两翼。精锐士卒,用来突破敌阵、擒杀敌将。
强弩劲射,用于激烈持久的战斗。飘风阵
⋯⋯。普通士卒用来分担任务、协助取胜。"孙
膑说:"贤明的君主和通晓用兵规律的将帅,是
不寄希望于用众多的普通士卒建功立业的。"
孙膑出来后,弟子们问他:"威王、田忌君
臣二人所提的问题怎样?"孙膑说:"威王
问了九个问题,田忌问了七个问题,他们接近

of a cone formation is to break through a solid position and destroy the enemy crack troops. The function of a wild geese formation is to attack the enemy in a pincer movement. The function of crack contingents is to break through the enemy formation and capture enemy generals. The function of powerful archery units is to sustain a fierce and long battle. The function of a wind formation is.... The rank-and-file troops are used to take up auxiliary tasks and help in winning victory. But wise sovereigns and capable commanders do not place their hopes on the use of large numbers of rank-and-file troops to accomplish great tasks."

When Sun Bin came out from the consultation, his disciples asked what he thought of the questions posed by King Wei and Tian Ji. Sun Bin said, "King Wei asked nine questions while Tian Ji asked seven. They are getting closer to under-

【原文】

兵矣,而未达于道也。吾闻素信者昌,立义
……用兵无备者伤,穷兵者亡。齐三世其忧
矣。"

* * *

……善则敌为之备矣。"孙子曰……

……孙子曰:"八阵已阵……

……□孙子曰:"毋待三日□……

……也。孙子曰:"战……

……□威王曰……

……道也。"田忌……

【今译】

于懂得用兵了,但还没有到达掌握用兵规律的
地步。我听说,一贯守信用,国家就昌盛。树
立正义……。进行战争而没有充分准备,国家
就会受到损害。穷兵黩武,国家必然灭亡。再
过三代,齐国的命运就令人忧虑了。"

standing the art of war, but they have not yet mastered it. I have heard it said that a state prospers when its rulers consistently stick to their words and uphold justice.... The state, which wages war without proper preparation, will suffer and the state, which is warlike, will perish. Three generations from now is really when one need to worry about the fate of Qi."

陈忌问垒

【原文】

陈忌问垒

田忌问孙子曰："吾卒少不相见,处此若何?"曰:"传令趣弩舒弓,弩□□□□□……不禁,为之奈何?"孙子曰:"明将之问也。此者人之所过而不急也。此□之所以疾……志也。"田忌曰:"可得闻乎?"曰:"可。用此者,所以应猝窘处隘塞死地之中也。是吾所以取

【今译】

田忌问孙膑说:"我军士卒少彼此联系不上,处于这种情况应该怎么办?"又说:"传令士卒赶快张弩引弓,……不能禁止,该怎么办呢?"孙膑说:"这是明智的将领所提的问题。这是一般人容易忽略过去而不重视的。……"田忌说:"可以讲来听听吗?"孙膑说:"可以。这是用以对付突然陷于窘迫处境和险隘阻塞之地的敌人的,也是我挫败庞涓、俘

Tian Ji 's Inquiries
Concerning Ramparts

Tian Ji asked Sun Bin, "What shall I do if my troops are few and have lost contact with each other?" He asked further, "What should I do after I have already ordered the troops to use their crossbows and arrows... and I cannot then recall the order?"

Sun Bin said, "These are the kinds of questions capable generals would ask and which ordinary people would usually overlook or pay little attention to...."

But Tian Ji persisted, "Will you be more specific?" "I shall," said Sun Bin. "This is the method used in dealing with the enemy which is suddenly faced with a dilemma or closed in by narrow passes. It is what I used to defeat Pang Juan and

【原文】

庞〔□〕而擒太子申也。"田忌曰："善。事已往而形不见。"孙子曰："蒺藜者,所以当沟池也。车者,所以当垒〔也〕。〔□□者〕,所以当堞也。发者,所以当俾倪也。长兵次之,所以救其隋也。钑次之者,所以为长兵〔□〕也。短兵次之者,所以难其归而邀其衰也。弩次之者,所以当投机也。中央无人,故盈之以□……卒已定,乃具其法。制曰:以弩次蒺藜,

【今译】

获太子申时所使用的方法。"田忌说："很好。事情已经过去,当时的情形已看不见了。"孙膑说："蒺藜,可以权且用来起护城河的作用。战车,可以权且用来起壁垒的作用。〔车箱〕可以权且用来起城上矮墙的作用。盾牌,可以权且用来起有孔矮墙的作用。长柄兵器依次排列,是用来援救危急之处的。配置车、矛等武器装备,是用来辅助长兵器的。配置短兵器,是用来断敌归路、阻击疲惫之敌的。配置弩兵,是用来灵活机动地打击敌人的。……以上各项都达到了,便具备了城垒作战

capture Prince Shen."

Tian Ji said, "Fine, but all that belongs to the past and we cannot witness what took place then."

Sun Bin said, "Thorny obstacles can be used to form a makeshift moat and chariots can be used to form makeshift ramparts. Wagons can be used for embankments while shields can be used as low embankments. The rows of long-armed weapons can be used to render support in emergency cases. Other weapons can help too.... Following them are the short spears, which can serve to block the route of enemy retreat and intercept their worn-out troops. The archery units can serve to attack the enemy with mobility when circumstances warrant such action.... When the above are all in hand, then you will have the conditions to engage in a battle to defend the city with ramparts."

"*The Military Regulations* states: Place the

【原文】

然后以其法射之。垒上弩戟分。法曰：见使茱来言而动□……□去守五里置候，令相见也。高则方之，下则圆之。夜则举鼓，昼则举旗。"

＊ ＊ ＊

田忌问孙子曰："子言晋邦之将荀息、孙轸之于兵也，未□……

……无以军恐不守。"忌子曰："善。"田忌问孙子曰："子言晋邦之将荀息、孙……

……轸为晋要秦于殽，溃秦军，获三帅□……

……强晋，终秦缪公之身，秦不敢与……

……也，劲将之阵也。"孙子曰："士卒……

……田忌曰："善。独行之将也。……

【今译】

的条件。《制》说：把弓弩配置在蒺藜后面，然后按规定的距离和时机发矢射敌。壁垒之上，弩和戟要各占一半。《法》说：要等派出去刺探敌情的间谍回来报告情况……，要在离部队驻守之地五里远的地方设置观察哨，使之能与驻地保持联系。观察哨设在高处，就要建成方形；观察哨设在低处，就要建成圆形。夜间要用鼓声报警，白天则用旌旗信号进行联络。"

crossbows behind thorny bushes and direct the arrows at the enemy from designated distance and when the opportunity arises. When you get on top of the ramparts, use an equal number of crossbows and halberds."

"*The Military Rules* stipulates: Wait for the reports of the scouts who have been sent to find out the latest on the enemy's activities.... Set up observation posts five *li* away from where your troops are stationed and make sure that they maintain contact with you. When these posts are set up on high ground, they should be square in shape; when on low ground, they should be round in shape. During nighttime, drums should be used to sound an alarm, whereas in daytime flags should be used to establish liaison...."

【原文】

……人。"田忌请问兵情奈何……

……言而后中。"田忌请问……

……兵情奈何。孙子……

……请问兵伤□……

……见弗取。"田忌服问孙……

……□橐□□□焉。"孙子曰:"兵之□……

……□应之。"孙子曰:"伍□……

……□孙子曰:"□……

……□见之。"孙子……

……以也。"孙……

……□孙子……

……□明之吴越,言之于齐。曰知孙氏之道者,必合于天地。孙氏者……

……求其道,国故长久。"孙子……

……田忌请问知道奈何。孙子……

……而先知胜不胜之谓知道。已战而智其所……

……所以知敌,所以曰智。故兵无……

【今译】

* * *

……(此种兵法)被孙武运用于吴越,而被孙膑推布于齐国。懂得孙氏的兵法,行兵布阵必合于天地时宜……

172

* * *

"Master Sun's art of war was demonstrated in Wu and Yue and enunciated in Qi. Those who know his way will act in accord with heaven and earth...."

篡卒

【原文】

篡卒

　　孙子曰：兵之胜在于篡卒，其勇在于制，其
巧在于势，其利在于信，其德在于道，其富在于
亟归，其强在于休民，其伤在于数战。

　　孙子曰：德行者，兵之厚积也。信者，兵
明赏也。恶战者，兵之王器也。取众者，胜

【今译】

　　孙膑说：军事上的胜利在于选卒，作战勇
敢在于制度，作战灵活在于态势，军队坚强在
于诚信，素质优良在于教育，国家富足在于速
胜急归，国家强盛在于休养生息，国家衰弱在
于频繁征战。

　　孙膑说：优良的素质，是军队建设的坚实
基础。诚信，是军队中的信赏明罚。不好战，
是军事上的最高原则。取得士兵拥护，是胜

Selecting Crack Troops

Sun Bin said: "Winning military victories depends on the selection of crack troops. Bravery in battle depends on good regulations. Flexibility and mobility in war depend on strategic advantage. The effectiveness of an army depends on its integrity and trustworthiness. The quality of its troops depends on training and education. The prosperity of the state lies in the gaining of quick victories, its strength in enabling its people to rest and recuperate, and its decline in frequent expeditionary wars."

Sun Bin said: "The fine quality of an army provides it with a solid foundation. The army's trustworthiness is based on clear and impartial rewards and punishments. Dislike of war is the highest military principle. Winning the support of the soldiers is the sure guarantee of victory."

【原文】

□□□也。

孙子曰：恒胜有五：得主专制，胜。知道，胜。得众，胜。左右和，胜。量敌计险，胜。

孙子曰：恒不胜有五：御将，不胜。不知道，不胜。乖将，不胜。不用间，不胜。不得众，不胜。

孙子曰：胜在尽□，明赏，选卒，乘敌之

【今译】

利的保证。

孙膑说：经常打胜仗的条件有五个：得到君主信任有独立指挥权的，能胜利。懂得战争规律的，能胜利。得到士兵拥护的，能胜利。将帅之间同心协力的，能胜利。善于估量敌情、分析地形险易的，能胜利。

孙膑说，经常打败仗的原因有五个：受到君主控御的将帅，不能胜利。不懂得战争规律的，不能胜利。将帅不和的，不能胜利。不会使用间谍的，不能胜利。得不到士兵拥护的，不能胜利。

孙膑说：胜利的取得在于将帅能够忠于国家，奖赏严明，拥有选卒，善于乘敌之弊。

Sun Bin said: "There are five factors leading to constant victory: A commander who has the trust of his sovereign and can direct his battles independently wins; one who knows the way of war wins; one who has the support of his soldiers wins; one who can unite his subordinates wins; and one who is adept at analyzing the enemy and sizing up the terrain wins."

Sun Bin said: "There are five factors leading to frequent defeat: A commander who is constrained by his sovereign loses; one who does not know the way of war loses; one who is at cross purposes with his generals loses; one who does not know how to use spies loses; and one who does not have the support of his soldiers loses."

Sun Bin said: "Victory depends on the loyalty of the commander and his generals to their country, on strict adherence to principle in handing out rewards, on the selection of crack troops and on the ability to exploit the weaknesses of the enemy. These are the magic weapons which give

【原文】

□。是谓泰武之葆。

孙子曰:不得主弗将也。……

* * *

……□□令,一曰信,二曰忠,三曰敢。安忠? 忠王。安信? 信赏。安敢? 敢去不善。不忠于王,不敢用其兵。不信于赏,百姓弗德。不敢去不善,百姓弗畏。

二百卅五

【今译】

这是使军队强大的法宝。

孙膑说:得不到君主的信任,是不能率兵任将的,……

an army its prowess and strength."

Sun Bin said: "He who does not have the trust of his sovereign should not assume command of the army."

月　　战

【原文】

月战

　　孙子曰:间于天地之间,莫贵于人。战
□□□人不战。天时、地利、人和,三者不得,
虽胜有殃。是以必付与而□战,不得已而后

【今译】

　　孙膑说:在天地之间,没有比人更宝贵的。
……天时、地利、人和,三个条件如果不完全具
备,即使取得了胜利也会有祸患。因此,必须
符合天时、地利、人和这三个条件才
能出战,不得不战才去作战。所以能够遵循

The "Heaven" Factor
in War

Sun Bin said: "Between heaven and earth there is nothing more precious than human beings.... Favors bestowed by heaven and earth, and the harmony of people (*tr.* : *meaning support of the people*) — when these three conditions are not all present, you will be courting trouble even if you have won victory. Therefore, go into battle only when you possess all three conditions; go into war only when there is no alternative. That is why he who fights with the favors of heaven does

【原文】

战。故抚时而战,不复使其众。无方而战者小胜以付屠者也。孙子曰:十战而六胜,以星也。十战而七胜,以日者也。十战而八胜,以月者也。十战而九胜,月有……〔十战〕而十胜,将善而生过者也。一单……

【今译】

天时而作战的,不需反复用兵。没有获得天时、地利、人和的全部有利条件,有时也取得一些小胜利,那是因为得到了天时中历数的帮助。孙膑说:十次作战而六次获胜,是因为得到了星德的有利条件。十次作战而七次获胜,是因为得到了日德的有利条件。十次作战而八次获胜,是因为得到了月德的有利条件。十次作战而九次获胜,……。十次作战而十次获胜,是因为将帅善于指挥,因而产生了超过天时作用的战果。

not have to fight repeatedly. When all these three favorable factors are not present, you may sometimes win minor victories, but that is only because you have the help of celestial sequence of events (*tr.: The ancients believed that the succession of empires and emperors was decided by celestial factors*). "

Sun Bin said: "When you win six out of ten battles, that is because you have the favors of the stars; when you win seven out of ten, that is because you have the favors of the sun; when you win eight out of ten, that is because you have the favors of the moon; when you win nine out of ten, that is because.... when you win all ten battles, that is because the commander is so adept at employing the troops that he secures results far exceeding the blessings of heaven...."

【原文】

* * *

……所不胜者也五,五者有所壹,不胜。故战之道,有多杀人而不得将卒者,有得将卒而不得舍者,有得舍而不得将军者,有覆军杀将者。故得其道,则虽欲生不可得也。

八十

【今译】

* * *

……不能取胜的因素有五种,五种之中有一种,就不能取胜。作战中经常出现的情形是:有的能杀伤许多敌人士兵而不能俘获敌人的将吏,有的能俘获敌人的将吏而不能袭占敌人的营舍,有的能袭占敌人的营舍而不能俘获敌军的将领,有的既能歼灭敌人全军又能击杀敌军将领。因此,只要掌握了战争规律,敌人想要逃避失败的命运也是不可能的。……

* * *

" . . . . There are five factors for not winning. Any one of the five is enough to ruin a battle."

"Frequently the following situations arise during battles: Sometimes you inflict heavy casualties on the enemy but fail to capture his officers and soldiers; sometimes you capture the enemy officers and soldiers but fail to seize their camps; sometimes you occupy their camps without capturing their commander; and sometimes you annihilate the entire army including its commander and generals. Once you have mastered the art of war, the enemy will not be able to escape the fate of defeat no matter how hard he tries."

八　阵

【原文】

八阵

　　孙子曰:智不足,将兵,自恃也。勇不足,将兵,自广也。不知道,数战不足,将兵,幸也。夫安万乘国,广万乘王,全万乘之民命者,唯知道。知道者,上知天之道,下知地之理,内得其民之心,外知敌之情,阵则知八阵

【今译】

　　孙膑说:智谋不足的人带兵打仗,是自负。勇气不足的人带兵打仗,是自大。不懂用兵规律而又缺乏多次作战经验的人带兵打仗,是希图侥幸取胜。凡是要巩固万乘大国的地位,扩大万乘大国的影响,保护万乘大国的人民生命安全,就必须掌握战争的规律。掌握战争规律,就是要上懂天文,下懂地理,内得民心,外知敌情,布阵要懂得八阵的要

Setting up Formations

Sun Bin said:

"A commander who lacks wisdom yet engages in war suffers from self-conceit. One who lacks courage yet does so suffers from arrogance. One who does not know the art of war and lacks battle experience relies on chance to achieve victory."

"It is imperative for one who wants to consolidate the position of a major power commanding 10,000 chariots, expand its influence and protect the security of its people to learn the art of war. And he who has mastered this art knows the way of heaven and earth, has the support of the populace and is fully aware of the enemy's situation. When he needs to determine his battle array, he

【原文】

之经,见胜而战,弗见而诤。此王者之将也。

孙子曰:用八阵战者,因地之利,用八阵之宜。用阵三分,诲阵有锋,诲锋有后,皆待令而动。斗一,守二。以一侵敌,以二收。敌弱以乱,先其选卒以乘之。敌强以治,先其下

【今译】

领,有胜利把握就打,没有胜利把握就不打。这样的统帅,才是能够帮助国君安邦定国的良将。

孙膑说:运用八阵作战,必须根据地形的有利条件,因地制宜地部署八阵。布阵时兵力要分为三个单元方阵,每个单元方阵都要有前锋部队,每一支前锋部队都要有后卫做应援,前锋和后卫都要待命而动。突击用一个单元的兵力,机动用两个单元的兵力。用一个单元进攻,用两个单元殿后。敌军战斗力弱而且阵势混乱,就先用选卒去乘敌之隙。敌军战斗力强而且阵势严整,就要先用战斗

knows how to set up the formations. He fights when there is assurance of victory, he stops fighting when there isn't. Such a commander is a true general worthy of his sovereign."

Sun Bin said:

"In deciding your battle formations, it is necessary to pay attention to the favourable features of the terrain and set up your formation accordingly. Your forces should be divide into three units; each unit should have a vanguard and each vanguard a rear force. Both the vanguard and rearguard must act under orders in all their movements. For every unit of the assault force, there must be two reserve units to give it support. When the enemy is weak and his formations confused, use crack troops to attack his weak points; when the enemy is strong and his formations orderly, lure it out with weak forces first. When

【原文】

卒以诱之。车骑与战者,分以为三,一在于右,一在于左,一在于后。易则多其车,险则多其骑,厄则多其弩。险易必知生地、死地,居生击死。

二百一十四

八阵

【今译】

力弱的部队去引诱它。有车兵和骑兵参加作战时,也要分为三部分,一部分部署在右翼,一部分部署在左翼,一部分部署在后卫。地形平坦时要多用车兵,地形险要时要多用骑兵,地形隘塞时要多用弩兵。无论地形险隘还是平坦,都要掌握哪里是有利的生地,哪里是不利的死地,占据有利的生地,击敌于不利的死地。

your chariots and cavalry take part in the battle, divide them into three units, one on the right flank, one on the left and one in the rear. Where the battleground is level, use mostly chariots; where it is rough and dangerous, use mostly cavalry; where there are narrow passes, use mostly the archery unit. No matter what type of ground you have, whether it is difficult of access or not, it is always necessary to know where the terrain is favourable and where it is hazardous, the latter being sometimes a point of no return. Occupy the favourable terrain and strike at the enemy when he is at such a point."

地　葆

【原文】

　　孙子曰:凡地之道,阳为表,阴为里,直者为纲,术者为纪。纪纲则得,阵乃不惑。直者毛产,术者半死。凡战地也,日其精也,八风将来,必勿忘也。绝水、迎陵、逆流、居杀地、迎众树者,钩举也,五者皆不胜。南阵之山,

【今译】

　　孙膑说:地形的一般状况是,向阳处为表,背阴处为里;大路为纲,小路为纪。掌握了大小道路的分布情况,出兵布阵就不会迷惑。大路对军事行动有利,蜿蜒曲折的小路对军事行动带来诸多不便。在作战地区,日照条件极为重要,对风向、风力的变化也切不可忘记观察。渡水、面朝丘陵、面迎上游、地处极不利的地形、面向树林这五种情境,都对作战不利,都可能战败,都应当离

Significance of Ground

Sun Bin said:

"Generally speaking, with respect to the various kinds of grounds, I regard the sunny side as the exterior and the shady side as the interior; the big roads as the major links and the paths as the minor links. He who knows the distribution of the roads and paths will not be confused when he sends his army to the battlefield and sets up his formations. Major roads are advantageous to military action while narrow winding paths pose many inconveniences."

"In areas of operation, it is very important to know whether there is sunshine or not. The observation of changes in wind direction and velocity should not be neglected either."

"Crossing a river, facing a hilly region, heading upstream, occupying an unfavorable terrain and facing a forest — these constitute the five situations which are unfavorable to military operations and which may lead to defeat. Therefore, both sides should try their best to avoid being placed in such situations."

【原文】

生山也。东阵之山,死山也。东注之水,生水也。北注之水,死水。不流,死水也。五地之胜曰:山胜陵,陵胜阜,阜胜陈丘,陈丘胜林平地。五草之胜曰:藩、棘、椐、茅、莎。五壤之胜:青胜黄,黄胜黑,黑胜赤,赤胜白,白胜青。五地之败曰:溪、川、泽、斥。五地之杀曰:天

【今译】

开远避。位于阵地北面的山,是有利的生山,位于阵地西面的山,是不利的死山。向东流的水,是生水。向北流的水,是死水。不流动的水,也是死水。五种作战地形也有优劣之分:山地优于高陵,高陵好于土山,土山胜于丘陵,丘陵胜于平地。五种植物生长的作战地形优劣比较是:丛树地最好,荆棘地次之,再其次是小乔木地和茅草地,最次的是莎草地。五种颜色的土壤,其优劣比较是:青土胜于黄土,黄土胜于黑土,黑土胜于红土,红土胜于白土,白土胜于青土。五种不利于作战的地形是:山涧、河流、沼泽、盐碱地〔和狭谷地〕。五种招致全军覆灭的地形是:四边陡峭

"A mountain of the north of the formation is 'life-giving', while one to the west is 'deadly'; a river which flows eastward is 'life giving' while one which flows northward is 'deadly'. Stagnant water is 'deadly' too."

"As far as fighting is concerned, the five kinds of terrain can be graded as follows: mountains are better than hills; wooded hills better than barren hills; barren hills better than rolling ground; and rolling ground better than wooded plains."

"Terrain can also be graded as follows according to five kinds of vegetations grown on it: woods are better than groves; groves better than brambles; brambles better than arbors and grass; arbors and grass better than nutgrass...."

"The earth has five colors. Their comparison is as follows: green earth is better than yellow earth, yellow better than black, black better than red, red better than white, while white is better than green."

"The following five types of terrain render operations difficult: ravines, rivers, marshes, alkaline land...."

"The following five types of terrain will surely

【原文】

井、天宛、天离、天隙、天柖。五墓,杀地也,勿居也。勿□也。春毋降,秋毋登。军与阵皆毋政前右,右周毋左周。

二百

地葆

【今译】

中间低洼积水的天井;四面环山、易进难出的天宛;草深林密、如同罗网的天离;沟坑交错、难以通过的天隙;地势低洼、道路泥泞的天柖。这五种地形称为五墓,是极不利的杀地。三军不可驻扎停留,不可排兵布阵。春夏不要在低处安营,因为春夏雨水较多;秋冬不宜在高处扎营,因为秋冬高处干燥缺水。军队驻扎和布阵不要让山陵位于自己的右前方,而右后方要有山陵高地环绕,左前方则不宜有高地环绕。

lead to the rout of the army: lowland surrounded
on all sides by precipices; areas surrounded by
mountains which are easy to enter and hard to get
out of; areas with groves of tress and tall grass
forming a sky net; chasms are full of ditches and
hollows, which making them impassable; lowland
and swamps where the roads are muddy. These
types of terrains are so unfavorable that they are
known as graveyards and it is not advisable for an
army to stop or set up formations there.... "

"During spring and summer, do not encamp on
lowland, for these are seasons when rainfall is
plentiful. During autumn and winter, do not encamp on highland, for there is a shortage of water
there during the dry season. Do not encamp or set
up formations with the highland to the right and
front nor be encircled by mountains to the left and
front. Rather choose to have the highland or
mountain encircle your camps on the right and
rear. "

势　备

【原文】

势备

孙子曰:夫陷齿戴角,前爪后距,喜而合,怒而斗,天之道也,不可止也。故无天兵者自为备,圣人之事也。黄帝作剑,以阵象之。羿作弓弩,以势象之。禹作舟车,以变象之。汤、武作长兵,以权象之。凡此四者,兵之用

【今译】

孙膑说:凡是长着锐齿、坚角、利爪、劲距的禽兽,欢喜时聚合在一起,发怒时就互相争斗。这是天性,不可制止。没有天生武器的人,就必须自己制造武器来自卫,这是圣人要做的事。黄帝制作宝剑,可以用军阵来比喻宝剑。后羿制作弓弩,可以用兵势来比喻弓弩。夏禹制作舟车,可以用机变来比喻舟车。商汤和周武王制作长柄兵器,可以用指挥权来比喻长柄兵器。以上阵、势、变、权四个方

Strategic Advantage

Sun Bin said:

"Animals which have sharp teeth, hard horns and fierce claws and spurs may come together when they are in good spirits but will fight each other when they are angry. That cannot be helped as it is in their nature to act so."

"Humans who lack these natural weapons have to devise arms to protect themselves. And this is the concern of the sages. Military formations may be compared to the sword, which the Yellow Emperor invented, strategic advantage to the bow and arrow, which Yi (*tr. : a tribal leader of the Xia Dynasty*) invented, contingency to the vessels and vehicles, which Yu of Xia invented, and authority to the halberd which Tang of the Shang Dynasty and King Wu of Zhou invented. These are all manifestations of the rules of war."

【原文】

也。何以知剑之为阵也？且暮服之，未必用也。故曰，阵而不战，剑之为阵也。剑无锋，虽孟贲〔之勇〕，不敢□□□。阵无锋，非孟贲之勇也敢将而进者，不知兵之至也。剑无首铤，虽巧士不能进〔□〕□。阵无后，非巧士敢将而进者，不知兵之情者。故有锋有后，相信不动，敌人必走。无锋无后……□券不道。

【今译】

面都是军事规律的反映。为什么说宝剑好比军阵呢？早晚都要佩戴着宝剑，但不一定使用它。所以说，布阵而不打仗，宝剑就如同军阵了。宝剑如果没有锋刃，即使像孟贲那样勇猛，也不敢〔用以上阵杀敌〕。军队如果没有前锋，又没有孟贲那样的勇士，还硬要向敌人发动进攻，这样的指挥者是最不懂用兵之道的。宝剑如果没有把柄，即使再精干的人也无法拿它刺杀敌人。军队如果没有后卫，又没有精兵，还硬要向敌人攻击，这样的指挥者也是不懂得用兵的实质的。所以，军阵既要有前锋，又要有后卫，阵势稳固，敌人必然会败走。如果军阵既无前锋又无后卫〔是违

"Why do I compare military formation to the sword? Because just as we wear the sword day and night even though we need not use it, we also set up formations even though we are not always engaged in battle. This is how the formation resembles the sword. A sword, which does not have a sharp edge, is useless. For even a brave man like Meng Ben dares not use it in battle. Take an army that does not have a vanguard and does not have brave fighters like Meng Ben, and yet launches an attack against the enemy-anyone who commands such an army knows nothing about the art of war. Similarly, a commander is ignorant of the art of war if he orders his army to attack the enemy without first preparing a rearguard, for the rearguard is like the handle of a sword without which the sword is useless."

"Hence, an army must have a vanguard and a rearguard, and so long as the formation is solid, it will put the enemy to rout without fail. To organize an army without a rearguard and a vanguard goes against the basics of the art of war...."

【原文】

何以知弓弩之为势也？发于肩膺之间,杀人百步之外,不识其所道至。故曰,弓弩势也。何以〔知舟车〕之为变也？高则……何以知长兵之权也？击非高下非……□卢毁肩。故曰,长兵权也。凡此四……所循以成道也。知其道者,兵有功,主有名。□用而不知其道者,〔兵〕无功。凡兵之道四：曰势,曰变,曰

【今译】

背军事原则的〕。怎么可以用弓弩比喻兵势呢？箭镞在肩膀和胸前射出,却可以在百步之外杀伤敌人,而敌人还不知道箭是从哪里射来的。所以说,弓弩好比兵势。为什么说可以用舟车比喻军队的机变呢？……为什么说可以用长柄兵器比喻作战主动权呢？长兵器可以在较远的距离上上下左右自由地击刺,……可以击刺敌人的头颅和肩膀。所以说,长柄兵器好比是作战指挥的主动权。……懂得战争规律,战争能取胜,君主有威名。但是,作战而不懂作战规律的人,打不了胜仗。用兵作战的规律是四条：叫做阵、势、

"Why do I compare strategic advantage to the bow and arrow? Arrows are shot from between the shoulder and the breast but they can kill an enemy 100 paces away often without his knowing where they come from. That is why I say strategic advantage is like the bow and arrow."

"Why do I compare contingency to vessels and vehicles?..."

"Why do I compare authority to long armed weapons? These weapons can be thrust in all directions and from a distance. They strike right at the enemy's head and shoulders. That is why I compare authority, which implies initiative in war, to long armed weapons...."

"He who knows the art of war will fight and win, thus bringing his sovereign power and fame. He who does not will fight and lose. There are four musts when fighting a war. These are: formation, strategic advantage, contingency and authority. He who masters these four musts

【原文】

阵,曰权。察此四者,所以破强敌,取猛将也。……势者,攻无备,出不意……中之近……也,视之近,中之远。权者,昼多旗,夜多鼓,所以送战也。凡此四者,兵之用也。

□皆以为用,而莫彻其道。

* * *

……□得四者生,失四者死,□□□□……

【今译】

变、权。深刻理解这四条原则,就能够打败强敌,生擒猛将,……兵势,就是攻其无备,出其不意。……战场指挥,就是白天用旌旗,夜间用金鼓,用以指挥作战。以上四条,都是军事原则的具体体现,人们都在应用它,却没有通晓它的道理。

will defeat his enemy and even capture its brave generals...."

"Strategic advantage is to attack the enemy when he least expects you, catching him unprepared.... In the battlefield authority implies knowing how to use flags and banners during the day and drums during the night when directing battles in the field...."

"These four musts are concrete applications of the art of war. Many use them but do not know the whys and wherefores."

〔兵 情〕

【原文】

孙子曰:若欲知兵之情,弩矢其法也。矢,卒也。弩,将也。发者,主也。矢,金在前,羽在后,故犀而善走。前〔重而〕后轻,故正而听人。今治卒则后重而前轻,阵之则办,趣之敌则不听人,治卒不法矢也。弩者,将

【今译】

孙膑说,如果想要了解用兵的道理,可以用弩矢作比喻。矢,好比是士卒。弩,好比是将帅。射手,好比是国君。矢的构造,箭头在前,箭羽在后,所以射出去以后强劲有力而且飞快。箭矢前重而后轻,所以能按照射手的意愿正确运行。现在治军是后重前轻,用来布阵还可以,用于赴敌就难以听从指挥了,这是由于人们治军时没有效法弩矢的缘故。

How to Run an Army

Sun Bin said:

"If you want to know how to run an army, all you have to do is to find out how the crossbow and arrow work. The arrow is like the soldiers, the crossbow the commander and the archer the sovereign. The metal head is at the front of the arrow and the feathers at the back. That is why when the drawn crossbow is released, the arrow flies out at great speed. Since the arrow head is heavy, the arrow moves in the direction the archer wants it to move."

"Nowadays, some people run the army light at the head and heavy in the rear. That may be all right when they set up formations, but when the troops go into combat, such an arrangement simply won't work. This is because they have not followed the example of the crossbow and the arrow

207

【原文】

弩,好比是将帅。弩弓张开后如果弩柄不正,
也。弩张柄不正,偏强偏弱而不和,其两洋之
送矢也不壹,矢虽轻重得,前后适,犹不中〔招
也〕,……□□□将之用心不和……得,犹不胜
敌也。矢轻重得,前〔后〕适,而弩张正,其送矢
壹,发者非也,犹不中招也。卒轻重得,前后
适,而将唯于……兵□□□□□□□犹不
胜敌也。故曰,弩之中彀合于四,兵有功

【今译】

就会一侧偏强一侧偏弱而不协调,它的两端对
箭的推动力就不一致,这样,箭矢虽然轻重得
当,前后适宜,也还是射不中箭靶。……将领
之间不协调一致,……也不能战胜敌人。箭矢
轻重比例得当,前后位置适宜,弩臂张得也端
正,弩弓两翼弹射箭矢的力量也一致,但射手
射艺不行,还是不能射中靶子。部署兵力主次
比例得当,前后位置适宜,……也不能战胜
敌人。所以说,发射弩箭要射中箭靶,必

when running an army."

"The crossbow is like the commander; when the bow is drawn, if the trigger is not shaped properly, if one side is heavier and stronger than the other, then the two sides will not have the same propelling force and the arrow will not hit the target. Similarly when the generals do not coordinate with each other... there will be no victory over the enemy."

"Even when the arrow is correctly made, the bow string rightly drawn and the two segments of the string are even in strength, if the archer is not skilled at shooting, he still will miss the target."

"When the commander deploys his troops, his main and auxiliary forces must be suitably apportioned, so must the positioning of the vanguard and the rearguard. Otherwise, the army still cannot win.... To hit the target when shooting an arrow, one must meet the above-mentioned four requirements. To fight a successful battle, one has to have the right mix of commander, officers

【原文】

……将也,卒也,□也。故曰,兵胜敌也,不异于弩之中招也。此兵之道也。

【今译】

须符合以上四个方面的要求,……所以说,军队战胜敌人的道理,与弩箭射中靶子的道理没有什么不同。这就是用兵之道。

and men...."

"That is why I say, there is really no difference between the way an army vanquishes its enemy and the way the crossbow arrow hits its target. Herein lies the secret to running an army."

行 篡

【原文】

行篡

　　孙子曰:用兵移民之道,权衡也。权衡,所以选贤取良也。阴阳,所以聚众合敌也。正衡再累……既中,是谓不穷。称乡悬衡,虽其宜也。私公之财壹也。夫民有不足于寿而有余于货者,有不足于货而有余于寿者,唯明王、圣人知之,故能

【今译】

　　孙膑说:"指挥军队、动员民众的道理,好比用天平衡量轻重。衡量轻重,是为了更好地选取人才。占卜阴阳,是为了聚集兵力与敌人交战。反复斟酌,不断平衡,至公至平,这叫做无穷无尽。选定方向,衡量利弊,寻求一个适当的标准。私财公产从根本上说是一体的。老百姓有富有而贪生的,有贫穷而不吝惜生命的。唯有贤明的国君和圣哲的人懂得这个道理,所以能驱使他们。为战

Making the Right Choice

Sun Bin said:

"In running an army and in mobilizing the populace, you must constantly weigh the pros and cons in order to make the right choice. You try to find the *yin* and *yang* of things so as to judge what is the best way to assemble the troops to fight the enemy. You weigh the pros and cons and try to strike the right balance so that your choice will be fair and impartial. Since the process never ends, you need to choose the right direction and weigh the advantages and disadvantages before you can arrive at the right conclusion."

"In the final analysis, private and public properties are used for the same purpose. Among the populace, there are those who are rich but who cravenly cling to life and those who are poor but who are not afraid to die. Only the wise sovereigns and sages understand this, and thus know

【原文】

留之。死者不毒，夺者不愠。此无穷……□□□□民皆尽力，近者弗则，远者无能。货多则辨，辨则民不德其上。货少则□，□则天下以为尊。然则为民赇也，吾所以为赇也。此兵之久也，用兵之国之宝也。

【今译】

斗而牺牲的人不怨恨，丢掉官职的人不抱怨。〔这样，财物会无穷无尽〕，民众都会竭力效命，与长官亲近的人不敢为非作歹，与长官疏远的人不敢松懈怠慢。征收财物多，民众就会受损，受损的民众就会不拥护国君；征收财物少，国君就会受到尊重。然而，征收财物就是为民众聚集财富，我们所以为民众聚集财富，这是因为战争要长期进行……

how to administer them. Then, in a war, those who sacrifice their lives in battle have no regret nor rancour, and those who have to give up their possessions have no grievances. Hence, an endless supply... and the populace will do everything to serve the cause. Those close to the officials dare not run roughshod over others and those distant to the officials dare not relax their efforts."

"The higher the taxes and levies, the greater the suffering of the populace, and the less their support for the sovereign. The lower the taxes and levies, the greater the populace's respect for the sovereign. However, in the final analysis, taxation is levied to collect riches for the populace and the reason there is a need for this is simple — the war has to go on for a long time...."

杀　士

【原文】

杀士

　　孙子曰:明爵禄而……

……士死。明赏罚□……

……士死。立□……

……必审而行之,士死。……

……死。桥而下之,士死。□……

……之,士死。□而傅……

……勉之欢,或死州□……

……之亲,或死坟墓……

……之鸤,或死饮食……

……□处之安,或死疾痎之间,或死……

【编者按】

　　本篇简文残缺过多,无法释译成现代汉语,也无法英译。谨存残简。

　　从篇题及残简看,竹简整理小组认为本篇主要内容是讨论将帅如何才能让士卒为之效命;本书校释者则认为本篇似是讨论精简士卒。

Troops Reduction

Editors ' Note: It is impossible to decipher the text of this chapter and translate it into modern Chinese as too many characters on the bamboo strips are either missing or unrecognizable. The restoration team is of the opinion that this chapter probably discussed how generals should mobilize his troops to fight to the bitter end. Yet, the compilers of this book think this chapter dealt with the streamlining of troops.

延　气

【原文】

延气

　　孙子曰:合军聚众,〔务在激气〕。复徙合军,务在治兵利气。临境近敌,务在厉气。战日有期,务在断气。今日将战,务在延气。……以威三军之士,所以激气也。将军令……其令,所以利气也。将军乃……短衣絜裘,

【今译】

　　孙膑说:编组军队聚集军需,务必要激励士气。连续行军、到达集结地区,务必要整饬武器装备,振奋部队精神。兵临边境、接近敌人,务必要鼓舞士气。战期已定,务必要造成决一死战的士气。在交战这一天,务必要能够保持持久的高昂士气。……用以威震全军士卒,这就是激发士气的方法。将军命令……的命令,是造成有利士气的方法。将军……身着短衣粗服,以鼓舞士卒的斗志,这就

Sustaining Morale

Sun Bin said:

"Having assembled an army and collected the provisions, [you need to sustain the morale of the troops]. After arriving at the assembly point following a continuous march, you need to have the arms and equipment in good order and raise the troops' morale. As the army approaches the border and gets close to the enemy, the troops must be in high spirits. When the time for launching the attack is decided, there must be a will to fight to win, whatever the sacrifices. On the day of the battle, it is absolutely indispensable to sustain their fighting spirit... to have something to inspire the troops that is a way to boost their morale....

"An order issued by the commander is... a means to boost their morale. By wearing the simple, coarse uniform of the soldiers, the commander

【原文】

以劝士志,所以厉气也。将军令,令军人人为
三日粮,国人家为……望,国使毋来,军使毋
往,所以断气也。将军召将卫人者而告之曰:
饮食毋……〔所〕以延气……也。

延气

* * *

……营也。以易营之众而贵武敌,必败。
气不利则拙,拙则不及,不及则失利,失利……
……气不厉则慑,慑则众□,众……
……气不断则迥,〔迥〕则不搏易散,临难
易散必败。……
……□□气不□则惰,惰则难使,难使则
不可以合旨……
……□□则不知为已之节,不知为已之节
则事……
……□而弗救,身死家残,将军召使而勉
之,击……

【今译】

是激励士气的方法。将军命令,全军每人携带
三天的口粮,……朝廷不再派使者到军队来,
军队也不派使者到朝廷去,这是造成断然决战
的士气的方法。……

makes them feel excited and keeps them in high spirits.

"By ordering the soldiers to carry with them only three days' supplies... by telling them that the messengers from the court are no longer expected and the army is not sending any more messengers to the court — that gives the impression a decisive battle is about to take place and readies the soldiers for it...."

官 一

官一

　　孙子曰：凡处卒利阵体甲兵者，立官则以身宜，贱令以采章，乘削以伦物，序行以〔□〕□，制卒以州间，授正以乡曲，辨疑以旌舆，申令以金鼓，齐兵以从迹，庵结以人雄，邋军以索阵，茭肆以囚逆，陈师以危□，射战以云阵，

【今译】

　　孙膑说：凡是屯驻军队、排兵列阵、配置兵器、设官立职都要如人的身体一样统一协调，要按不同的军衔传达命令，用旌旗区分战车的等级，……按州、间地方行政单位组建军队，根据地方行政区划任命军队长官，用各色旗帜区分不同的建制单位，用金、鼓下达命令，用步伐来整齐部队行列，用勇猛的士兵担任护卫，用"索阵"来进剿敌军，用"囚逆阵"来反复疲惫敌人，用"云阵"与敌人进行弩弓交

The Officer's Functions

Sun Bin said:

"When taking measures such as stationing troops, assuming battle formations, distributing weapons and appointing officers, you must coordinate them as if they are all parts of the same human body. Commands must be passed down according to ranks and the chariots must be differentiated by the different banner colors.... Detachments must be set up according to different regional administrations and their officers appointed in the same way. The different units must be distinguished from each other by different banner colors. Orders must be given by using the gongs and the drums. Troops on the march must advance with uniform steps. They must be covered by brave fighters. Use the *suo* formation (*tr.*: *The indicates that the meaning is not clear. The same applies to other asterisks in this chapter.*) to attack the enemy and the *qiuni* formation to exhaust him. When there is an exchange of crossbow arrows, use the *yun* formation. Counter

【原文】

御裹以羸渭，取喙以阖燧，即败以包□，奔救以皮傅，燥战以错行。用□以正□，用轻以正散，攻兼用行城……

□地□□用方，迎陵而阵用刲，险□□□用圜，交易武退用兵，□□陈临用方……

翼，氾战接厝用喙逢，囚险解谷以□远，草驵沙荼以阳削，战胜而阵以奋国，而……

【今译】

射战斗，用"赢渭阵"来抵御敌人的包围，用"阖燧阵"来歼灭敌军前锋，用"皮傅阵"来奔救友军，用"错行阵"鼓噪而战。……用轻装部队征剿残敌，用"行城"攻占敌人的城邑。……

……，面向高陵布阵要用"刲阵"，……，在畅通无阻、地势平坦之处撤军要用兵力掩护，……

……一般战斗，在短兵相见时要充分发挥前锋的作用，制敌于山险中要放开谷口以引敌出险再消灭之，在杂草丛生地带行军要预先打开视角开阔的通道，打了胜仗要严饬阵容以振国威，……

the enemy encirclement with *leiwei* formation (*probably a kind of extended formation — ed.*). Strike at the enemy vanguard with hesui formation (*probably a kind of formation that blocks roads and passes — ed.*). Rush reinforcements to friendly forces in need with *pifu* formation. Use *cuohang* formation (*probably a kind of staggered formation — ed.*) to clamour for battle.... Use a light brigade to annihilate the enemy remnants. Use *xingcheng* (*a kind of equipment that enables the troops to fight an enemy positioned at a high point — ed.*) when storming a walled city.... When confronted with enemy entrenched on high ground, use gui formation (*"gui" is a ceremonial jade object held by the kings of ancient times; it is shaped round at the top and square at the bottom — ed.*). When your troops have to withdraw on an open field, they must be covered....

"... Generally, when troops are engaged in hand-to-hand combat, the vanguard force has a special role to play. When the enemy is encircled in a narrow valley, draw him out of the mouth of the valley to annihilate him. When marching through land covered with tall grass, open up a way first to widen your vision. When a battle is won, the troops must resume neat formation to present the image of a victor...."

【原文】

为畏以山胠,秦怫以逶迤,便罢以雁行,险厄以杂管,还退以蓬错,绕山林以曲次,袭国邑以水则,辨夜退以明简,夜警以传节,厝入内寇以棺士,遇短兵以必舆,火输积以车,阵刃以锥行,阵少卒以合杂。合杂,所以御裹也。脩行连削,所以结阵也。云折重杂,所权

【今译】

……,在山岭弯曲处要布设"山胠阵",在荆棘杂草丛生之地要布"逶迤阵",疲惫敌人要用"雁行阵",在险厄之地要用"杂管阵",撤退时要用"蓬错阵",通过山林要用"曲次阵",袭击敌人的国都和城邑要以水流为法因敌制胜,辨别夜间撤退的部队要用明白清楚的书简,夜间警戒要严格检查通行凭证,突击或反突击要派武艺高强的人,与敌人短兵接战要密排战车,焚烧敌军的粮草辎重要用战车纵火,使阵势锋利要用"锥行阵",兵力不足要集中布阵。集中布阵,是为了反包围。整饬队伍布列旌旗,是为了妥善布阵。阵势如重叠

"When taking up position on a rugged section of a mountain, use the *shanqu* formation. When in ground covered with thickets and brambles, use the *weiyi* formation.... When trying to exhaust an enemy, use the *yanxing* formation. Use a *quci* formation when passing through a mountain forest. When attacking enemy cities and storming enemy capitals, follow the rule of water seeking its level. When your troops withdraw, use clearly written bamboo strips to identify the different detachments. When soldiers are put on night sentry, strict rules must be observed in the use of passwords. When making assaults, use brave and capable fighters. When fighting at close quarter, concentrate your chariots in close and serried ranks. Use the wagons to set the enemy provisions on fire. Use the cone formation to make your attack sharp and penetrating. When you are short of troops, concentrate them so that you can break out of enemy encirclement. Have the troops stand in order and arrange their banners accordingly so that you can set up a good formation."

【原文】

趡也。众风振陈,所以乘疑也。隐匿谋诈,所以钓战也。龙隋陈伏,所以山斗也。□□乖举,所以压津也。□□□卒,所以□□也。不意侍卒,所以昧战也。遏沟□陈,所以合少也。疏削明旗,所以疑敌也。剽阵辖车,所以从遗也。椎下移师,所以备强也。浮沮而翼,

【今译】

的阴云,是为了突击。阵如狂飙行进,是为了乘敌迷惑予以打击。隐蔽企图施用谋诈,是为了诱敌出战中我之计。强而示弱暗设伏兵,是为了诱敌进入山地战斗。……故意举动错谬,是为了引敌渡河以半济而击。……不把作战意图告诉士卒,是为了让他们盲目地拼死战斗。隔沟列阵,是为了以少敌众。疏列假兵器明设各种旗帜,是为了迷惑敌人。布列飘风阵,派出轻快战车,是为了追击逃窜之敌。摧垮敌军之后立即转移部队,是为了防备其它强敌。用浮沮阵猛扑敌军,是为了

"When readying for an assault, arrange your formations in layers thick as dark clouds. Make the formations advance with the momentum of a storm so as to render the bewildered enemy hard blows. Hide your intentions and use deceit to trick the enemy to meet you in battle. Pretend weakness and lay ambushes so as to draw the enemy into battle on the mountain.... Feign mistakes in your movement so as to lure the enemy to cross the river and attack it when it reaches midstream.... Do not inform the troops of your battle intentions so that they will fight to the finish. Assume a position behind a gully so that your few can counter the enemy's many. To confuse the enemy, litter the ground with useless weapons and banners. Arrange the troops in a *piaofeng* formation and send light chariots to overtake the fleeing enemy. When other powerful enemy forces are close by, move your troops away immediately after you have annihilated one enemy unit. Use

【原文】

所以燧斗也。禅祜虆避,所以莠槑也。简练剽便,所以逆喙也。坚阵敦□,所以攻槽也。揆断藩薄,所以眩疑也。伪遗小亡,所以饵敌也。重害,所以茭〔□〕也。顺明到声,所以夜军也。佰奉离积,所以利胜也。刚者,所以御劫也。更者,所以过□也。□者,所以御□也。□〔者,所以〕□□〔也。序〕者,所以厌门

【今译】

进行隧路战斗。不穿戴盔甲、行动不齐、故意示敌无备,是为了诱敌来追。选拔骁勇剽悍、熟练敏捷的士卒,是为了迎击敌人的前锋。布列坚阵、密集军队,是为了攻击敌军主力。毁掉用草木构成的篱障,是为了迷惑敌人。故意丢弃一些物资,是为了引诱敌人。多方陷敌于不利,是为了疲惫敌人。随着光亮,顺着声音是为了便于夜间作战。把各种军需物

the *fuju* formation to close in on the enemy so as
to force it to fight in 'tunnel' terrain, i.e., on a
road that is flanked by precipices."

"To make the enemy believe that you are unprepared, have your troops move about without
their amours and wander around in disorder. That
way you can lure him out to pursue you. To encounter the enemy vanguard, select the brave and
sturdy, the skilled and quick-witted, among your
soldiers. Assume a solid formation and concentrate your forces to attack the enemy's main
force. To confuse the enemy, destroy the obstacles made of grass and hedges. To lure the enemy, purposely abandon some of your positions.
To exhaust him, create all kinds of disadvantages
and inconveniences for him. Use light and sound
as your guide when fighting a night battle. To

【原文】

也。胡退□入,所以解困也。

* * *

……□令以金……

……云阵,御裹〔以赢渭,取喙〕以阖……

……荼以阳削,战……

……畏以山胑,秦怫以逶迤,便罢以雁

……夜退以明简,夜警……

……舆,火输积以车,阵……

……龙隋陈……

……也。疏削明……

……也。简练□便,所以逆喙也……

……断藩薄,所以眩〔疑也。伪遗小亡〕,

所以饵敌也。重害,所……

……奉离积,所以利……

……所以御□〔也。□者,所以□□〕也。

序者,所以厌……

【今译】

资分散存放,是为了利于取胜。配备战斗力强
的部队,是为了抵御敌人的袭击。……

make victory easier, store your military provisions
in different places. Keep some crack combat-ef-
fective troops on hand to protect yourself against
sneak attacks...."

五教法

【原文】

〔孙〕子曰:善教者于本,不临军而变,故曰五教:处国之教一,行行之教一,处军之〔教一,处阵之教一,隐而〕不相见利战之教一。处国之教奚如曰……孝弟良五德者,士无壹乎,虽能射不登车。是故善射为左,善御为

【今译】

孙膑说:善于教育训练的人对于最基本的条令条例,不会在临近安营布阵时随意更改,共分"五教":一种是在国内时的教戒,一种是在行军宿营时的教戒,一种是在军内的教戒,一种是在军阵中的教戒,一种是隐蔽以有利于作战时的教戒。在国内时的教戒是怎样的呢?称做……孝、悌、良五种好的品德,如果士卒一条也不具备,那么即使他们善于射箭也不能乘战车。所以善于射箭的当车

234

Five Ways to Train Troops

Sun Bin said:

"He who is adept at training does not change the army's basic rules and regulations when it is ready to encamp and set up formations. There are five ways of training:

"One, training in behavior in the home country; two, training for marches and encampment; three, training in rules and regulations within the army; four, training for battle formation; and five, training in the use of camouflage to facilitate fighting.

"What is training in behavior in the home country? This refers... to cultivating the five qualities of filial piety, love and respect for one's elder brothers, love and respect for one's spouse.... If a soldier does not possess any one of these qualities, he must not be allowed to mount the chariot even if he is a good archer. He who is adept at

【原文】

御,毕无为右。然则三人安车,五人安伍,十人为列,百人为卒,千人有鼓,万人为戎,而众大可用也。处国之教如此。行行之教奚如?废车疲马,将军之人必任焉,所以率……险幼将自立焉,所以敬□……□足矣。行行之教如

【今译】

左,善于驾车的当御手,射御都不会的当车右。三个车兵为一乘车的编制,五个步卒为一伍,十人为一列,一百人为一卒,每一千人设有指挥鼓,每一万人为一戎,便组成规模较大的可供使用的军队了。在国内时的教戒是这样。行军宿营时的教戒又是怎样的呢?战车破损,军马疲惫,率领军队的人必须承担责任,用以率……在遇到险要等不利条件时能自主处理……就足够了。行军宿营时的教

archery should be placed on the left-hand side, he who is adept at manipulating the chariot should be the driver and seated in the middle, and he who is adept at neither should be placed on the right. Three men are placed on a chariot, five men will form a *wu*, ten a *lie*, 100 a *zu*, every 1,000 men will form a unit provided with a commanding drum and 10,000 men form a *rong*. This will be sufficient to make a large contingent ready for deployment.

"Such being the training provided for the army when it is in the home country, what is the training for marches and encampments? If the chariots are ruined and the horses are exhausted, it is the commanding officers who must be held responsible.... When in danger or faced with an unfavorable situation, the troops must decide for themselves what to do...."

"Such is the training for troops in marches and encampments, what about training on rules and

【原文】

此。处军之教〔奚如?〕……也。处军之教如〔此。处阵〕之教奚如? 兵革车甲,阵之器也。……以兴善。然而阵既利而阵实蘩。处阵之教如此。隐而不相见利战之教〔奚如?〕……

五教法

* * *

……垒途道,使三军之士皆见死而不见生,所〔以〕……

……镢所以教耳也。……

……〔所〕以教足也。五教既至,目益明……

【今译】

戒是这样。在军内的教戒又是怎样的呢? ……在军内的教戒是这样。在军阵中的教戒又是怎样的呢? 武器装备是战阵中必不可少的器具。……振兴好的方面。这样便布列出有利的阵形和繁复的部署。处在军阵中的教戒是这样。隐蔽以有利于作战时的教戒又是怎样的呢? ……

regulations within the army?...

"What about training for battle formation?... Weapons and equipment are indispensable in forming battle formations... so as to give full play to their advantages. This will lead to the setting up of favorable formations and the use of intricate deployment. Such is the training for battle formation."

"What then is the training for the use of camouflage?...."

〔强　兵〕

【原文】

　　……威王问孙子曰:"□□□……□齐士教寡人强兵者,皆不同道。……〔有〕教寡人以政教者,有教寡人以〔□〕敛者,有教寡人以散粮者,有教寡人以静者,……〔孙子曰〕:"……皆非强兵之急者也。"威〔王〕……□□。

【今译】

　　威王问孙膑:"……齐国的学士教我强兵,各持不同的主见。……有的教我施仁政教化,……有的教我散粮于民众,有的让我清静无为……"孙膑说:"……这些都不是强兵最要紧的事。"威王问:"什么才是最要紧的事

Strengthening the Army

King Wei asked Sun Bin, "...Many scholars of Qi have advised me to strengthen the army, but they don't agree on how this can be done.... Some suggested that I practice a rule of benevolence..., others recommended I distribute grain and provisions among the populace. Still others have suggested that I let things run their course...."

To which Sun Bin replied, "None of these is the most crucial in strengthening the army."

King Wei [asked, "What then is the most crucial?"]

【原文】

孙子曰:"富国。"威王曰:"富国"。……□厚,

威王、宣王以胜诸侯,至于……

* * *

……将胜之,此齐之所以大败燕……

……众乃知之,此齐之所以大败楚人反

……

……知之,此齐之〔所以〕大败赵……

……□人于鄪桑而擒范皋也。

……擒唐□也。

……擒□罠。

【今译】

呢?"孙膑答道:"富国。"齐威王、宣王凭着富国

之道战胜了各国诸侯……

Sun Bin answered, "Make the country prosperous." When the King repeated these words, Sun Bin continued, "... it was by making the country prosperous that both King Wei and King Xuan defeated the neighboring states...."

附录：佚书辑录

Appendix:
Collection of Scattered Texts

十　阵

【原文】
十阵

　　凡阵有十：有方阵，有圆阵，有疏阵，有数
阵，有锥行之阵，有雁行之阵，有钩行之阵，有
玄襄之阵，有火阵，有水阵。此皆有所利。方
阵者，所以刲也。圆阵者，所以抟也。疏阵者，
所以吠也。数阵者，为不可掇。锥行之阵
者，所以决绝也。雁行之阵者，所以接射也。

【今译】
　　阵法有十种：方阵，圆阵，疏阵，数阵，锥形
阵，雁行阵，钩行阵，玄襄阵，火阵，水阵。

　　这些阵法都有它的长处。方阵，便于主将
统一指挥。圆阵，便于灵活运转。疏阵，用来
虚张声势。数阵，便于防止敌军分割。锥形
阵，用以突破敌阵切断敌群。雁行阵，便于

Ten Formations

There are ten kinds of formations: square, circular, loose, compact, cone, wild geese, hook, maze, fire and water. Each has its own advantages. The square formation is easy to direct. The circular provides greater mobility. The loose looks overwhelming and is beguiling. The compact prevents the enemy from breaking through. The cone is useful in breaking into enemy formation and reducing the adversary into pockets. The wild geese formation is convenient for shooting your arrows

【原文】

钩行之阵者,所以变质易虑也。玄襄之阵者,所以疑众难故也。火阵者,所以拔也。水阵者,所以伥固也。

　　方阵之法,必薄中厚方,居阵在后。中之薄也,将以吷也。重□其□,将以划也。居阵在后,所以……

　　〔圆阵之法〕……

【今译】

快速射击。钩行阵,利于改变敌人作战企图。玄襄阵,用以迷惑敌军,使其难于判明我军阵情。火阵,用以拔取敌人营寨。水阵,用以淹灌依城固守之敌。

　　方阵,须中间兵力少,四周兵力多,待机部队位置靠后。中间兵力少,用以虚张声势。〔四周兵力多〕用以粉碎敌军。待机部队位置靠后,便于灵活调动部队。

in rapid succession. The maze formation is used to confuse the enemy so that he is at a loss as to your troop deployment. The fire formation is used to destroy the enemy camp and the water formation to flood the enemy entrenched in a city.

When you use the square formation, concentrate your forces on the outside while placing few in the center, and the reserve is placed in the rear. The few troops in the center serve merely to make a show of strength while the forces on the outside are used to smash the enemy. The reason the reserve is placed in the rear is that it will be more agile.

The circular formation....

【原文】

〔疏阵之法〕,其甲寡而人之少也,是故坚之。武者在旌旗,是人者在兵。故必疏钜间,多其旌旗羽旄,砥刃以为旁。疏而不可戚,数而不可军者,在于慎。车毋驰,徒人毋趋。凡疏阵之法,在为数丑,或进或退,或击或颏,或与之征,或要其衰。然则疏可以取锐矣。

数阵之法,毋疏钜间,戚而行首,积刃而信之,前后相保,变□□□,甲恐则坐,以声坐

【今译】

疏阵是用于兵力少时坚固阵势的。可多设旌旗显示阵势威武,多竖武器显示人多。因此,应加大行列间的间隔,多竖各色旌旗羽旄,将光亮锋利的兵器布置在外侧。稀疏之阵应能收缩,密集之阵应能展开。如果不能收缩不能展开,就要谨慎。战车不可疾驰,步卒不可急走。疏阵的用法在于把兵力分成若干作战群体或进或退,或攻或守,或与敌军争夺阵地,或截击筋疲力尽的敌军。这样,疏阵就可以战胜精锐之敌了。

数阵的列法:行列间隔要小而密集,因此行列之首(排头兵)应多持兵刃,兵锋对敌。

The loose formation is used to consolidate your position when your forces are inferior in number to the enemy. You may set up a lot of banners to give a show of strength, flaunting your weapons ostensibly to indicate that you have a large force. Hence, you should maintain a distance between your ranks, display the multi-colored banners and put the shiny weapons up in front.

The loose ranks must be arranged in such a way that they can contract when necessary, while the close ranks must allow for extension. If the loose ranks cannot contract, and the close cannot extend, then great care should be taken to change the situation. The chariots must not speed too fast; the foot soldiers must not run. The secret of the success of the loose formation lies in dividing your forces into several independent units so that they can each advance or retreat, attack or defend, wrest the enemy's position or intercept the exhausted enemy as the situation requires. This way, the loose formation will succeed in overpowering even the enemy's crack troops.

The way to arrange the compact formation is to reduce the distance between the ranks. Therefore, the file leader, i.e., the soldier at the head of the line, should have his sword pointed at

【原文】

□,往者弗送,来者弗止,或击其迂,或辱其锐,笌之而无间,轵山而退。然则数不可掇也。

锥行之阵,卑之若剑,末不锐则不入,刃不薄则不刲,本不厚则不可以列阵。是故末必锐,刃必薄,本必鸿。然则锥行之阵可以决绝矣。

〔雁行之阵〕,……中,此谓雁阵之任。前

【今译】

前后要能相互支援。……如果士卒恐惧则稳定阵脚不动。敌人退去,不要出阵追击,敌军来犯时不要出阵阻击。或是截击其迂回部队,或挫折其前锋锐气。阵势要密得无隙可乘,敌如逢大山阻挡,被迫而退。这样的数阵,就不会被敌军攻破了。

锥形阵,好比一把利剑,前锋不锐利就不能突入敌阵,左右两翼不锋利,就不能切断敌军,主力不雄厚就无法成阵。所以前锋锐利,两翼锋利,主力雄厚。这样,锥形阵就可以突破和切断敌军了。

〔雁行阵〕:前锋部队要像大猩猩那样张

the enemy. There should be close coordination between the front and the rear.... Should the soldiers get frightened, it is important that you hold the ground.... When the enemy retreats, do not break up the formation to block him. You may intercept his troops sent to outflank you or deal a blow to his vanguard to dampen his spirit. Your formation should be arranged in such a way that it leaves no opening for the enemy to exploit and it will be forced to retreat as though its advance has been blocked by a mountain. Such a formation is unassailable.

The cone formation is like a sharp knife capable of cutting the enemy into pieces. If its vanguard is not sharp enough, it will not be able to break through the enemy formation. If its flanks are not swift enough, they will not be able to cut off the enemy. If its main force is not strong enough, it will not constitute a powerful formation. With a sharp front, swift flanks and a strong center, the cone formation is capable of penetrating the enemy's position and intercepting his forces.

In the wild geese formation, the vanguard should open its arms to embrace the enemy like

【原文】

列若馫,后列若狸,三……阙罗而自存,此之谓雁阵之任。

钩行之阵,前列必方,左右之和必钩。三声既全,五彩必具,辨吾号声,知五旗。无前无后,无……

玄襄之阵,必多旌旗羽旄,鼓罪罪庄,甲乱则坐,车乱则行,已治者□,樯樯唪唪,若从天下,若从地出,徒来而不屈,终日不拙。此之谓玄襄之阵。

【今译】

开两臂,环抱敌军,或抓住敌人,后卫部队像野猫那样猛扑上去,三面夹击,使敌不能突破罗网而自存,这就是雁行阵的作用。

钩行阵,正面部队列成方阵,左右两翼部队结成钩形。指挥所用的金、鼓、笳笛以及五色彩章齐全。使士卒能辨别号令,识别旗号。无论前面后面,指挥自如,无不得心应手……。

玄襄阵要多设旌旗羽旄,鼓声密集雄壮。士卒表面散乱而实际稳定;战车表面混乱而严整有序;故意发出兵车行进和士卒嘈杂喧嚣声,好像从天而降,从地而出,士卒往来穿梭,终日不绝。这就是玄襄阵。

a gorilla, and the rearguard will throw itself upon the enemy like a wild cat so that he cannot escape from the net cast on him. This is the function of the wild geese formation.

In the hook formation, the frontal units form a square while the flanks serve as hooks. All the instruments for passing down orders, such as gongs, drums and wind instruments, as well as coloured banners, must be on hand so that the soldiers can understand the orders and distinguish the banner signals. No matter where he is situated, the commander can direct his forces with ease. . . .

In the maze formation, there are lots of flags and banners while the drums beat ominously and incessantly. On the surface, the soldiers seem to be marching aimlessly when actually they are steady and firm; the chariots seem to be moving about at random when actually they are in perfect order. The thunderous clamors of troops and continuous rushing about of chariots create the impression that they have either descended from heaven or cropped up from the earth. Such is the maze formation.

【原文】

火战之法，沟垒已成，重为沟堑，五步积薪，必均疏数，从役有数，令人为属枇，必轻必利，风辟……火既自覆，与之战弗克，坐行而北。火战之法，下而衍以芥，三军之士无所出泄。若此，则可火也。陵＆蒋芥，薪荛既积，营窟未谨。如此者，可火也。以火乱之，以矢雨之，鼓噪敦兵，以势助之。火战之法。

【今译】

火攻的方法：深沟高垒筑成后，还要再挖些堑壕，每隔五步，堆放柴草，疏密而均匀。纵火的人不必多，令每人捆好纵火的草把，纵火时动作须敏捷利落，注意风向，避开下风，以免火殃自己，否则不但不能战胜敌人，反会因此而失败。若敌处下风，又在地势低而平坦、野草丛生的地带，火发时，敌军将士就无处可逃。在这种情况下，可用火攻。尤其是大风天气，敌军营地杂草丛生，柴草堆积，戒备不严，更可以用火攻。以猛烈的火势烧乱敌营，以密如雨的箭射杀敌人，击鼓呐喊，敲击兵器，督促士卒进攻，火助军威，兵趁火势，消灭敌军。这就是火战的方法。

The way to launch a fire attack is this: Having excavated deep gullies and built high ramparts, you need to dig trenches. Place firewood and straw at every five steps. There need not be too many fire setters. Each one holds a bunch of straw for lighting the fire, which they must do quickly. Pay close attention to the wind direction. Never stand downwind so as to avoid being burned yourself; otherwise, defeat, and not victory, will be your lot. When the wind is blowing towards the enemy, the ground is low and even and the region has plenty of grass, then the fire spreads and the enemy officers and men will have no way to escape. Such conditions are ideal for a fire attack. This is particularly so when you have a windy day, the enemy is unprepared and his camps are situated amidst reeds and with stockpiles of firewood around. Attack the enemy camp with fierce fire; shower his troops with arrows; beat the drums and strike the weapons, and clamour loudly so as to rouse your own soldiers to fall upon the enemy. With the momentum caused by the fire driving the soldiers forward, you will annihilate the enemy. Such is the way of the fire attack.

【原文】

水战之法，必众其徒而寡其车，令之为钩楷苁柤贰辑□绛皆具。进则必遂，退则不蹙，方蹙从流，以敌之人为招。水战之法，便舟以为旗，驰舟以为使，敌往则遂，敌来则蹙，推攘因慎而饬之，移而革之，阵而□之，规而离之。故兵有误，车有御徒，必察其众少，击舟颏津，示民徒来。水战之法也。

七百八十七

【今译】

水战的方法，必须多用步兵，少用战车，令部队把钩子、木筏、小船、叉子、轻船、桨、大船等各种水战用具都准备好。船队前进时须前后相随，后撤时不要相互拥挤，并船顺流而下，以敌军为射击目标。水上战斗的方法是：用轻便船只为指挥船，用快船进行联络，敌退则追击，敌进则迎战。进退都要根据情况慎重处理，使船队严整有序。敌船移动时则箝制它，敌列阵不动则袭击它，敌聚集兵力，则分割它。对水战中配置的车辆和步兵的数量，必须查清。攻击敌船，封锁渡口，调集步兵从陆地配合作战。这就是水战的方法。

The way to launch a water attack is this: use many foot soldiers but few chariots. Have the troops ready with handhooks, rafts, boats, forks, light boats, oars, ships and other equipment for a water attack. When the fleet moves forward, the ships must advance in a coordinated and orderly fashion; when it retreats, they must not crowd each other. The ships move downstream in parallel formation, shooting at the enemy as they sail past. In a water attack, use a light boat as the flagship and a fast boat for liaison; pursue the enemy when he flees, engage him when he advances. Care must be taken both in advance and in retreat so that the ships maintain an orderly formation. Tie the enemy down when he tries to move. Attack him when he is in formation and refuses to budge. Break him up when his ships are concentrated. Keep a clear account of the number of shovels and wagons (*tr.: needed for building dikes and channels to hold back the water during enemy inundation*) at your command. Have the foot soldiers attack enemy ships from the shore and, in coordination, blockade all ferry points. This is the method used in water attacks.

十　问

十问

兵问曰:交和而舍,粮食均足,人兵敌衡,
客主两惧。敌人圆阵以胥,因以为固,击〔之奈
何?曰〕:击此者,三军之众分而为四五,或
傅而佯北,而示之惧。彼见我惧,则遂分而不
顾。因以乱毁其固。驰鼓同举,五遂俱傅。

【今译】

兵家问道:两军对阵,双方粮食充足,兵力
兵器相当,彼此戒惧。敌军布成圆阵固守待
战,该如何攻击呢?

答:攻击这样的敌军,可将全军分成四五
路佯攻,与敌一接触就佯装败退,表示临阵畏
惧。敌军见我畏惧,就会不顾一切分兵追击,
这就打乱了它的坚固阵势。我军趋车击鼓并
举,五队兵马同时向敌逼近。五队兵马齐集

260

Ten Questions on Warfare

Question: Given that both sides are amply provisioned with food and other supplies, that they are equal in manpower and weapons and that they are vigilant and afraid of each other, how should we attack the enemy when he confronts us with a circular formation?

Answer: In dealing with such a formation, you may divide your forces into four or five detachments to simulate attack, and once they come into contact with the enemy, feign withdrawal to show fear and confusion. When the enemy finds that you are afraid, he will forget himself and, by following you in hot pursuit, he will scatter his forces. This will break up his solid formation. Then, you can beat the drums and draw your chariots together, and your five detachments will close in on the enemy simultaneously. When your forces are once again concentrated, they will

【原文】

五遂俱至,三军同利。此击圆之道也。

交和而舍,敌富我贫,敌众我少,敌强我弱,其来有方,击之奈何? 曰:击此者,□阵而□之,规而离之,合而佯北,杀将其后,勿令知之。此击方之道也。

交和而舍,敌人既众以强,劲捷以刚,锐阵以胥,击之奈何? 击此者,必三而离之,一

【今译】

后,三军同心协力进攻,夺取胜利。这就是破圆阵的方法。

问:两军对垒,敌军军需充足,我军军需缺少,敌众我寡,敌强我弱,敌军用方阵向我进攻,怎样抗击它呢?

答:抗击这样的敌军可用疏阵,分散它的兵力。一交战就佯装败退,然后调转兵力向敌军侧后进攻,不让敌军察觉我军意图。这是破方阵的办法。

问:两军对垒,敌军众多、强大、凶猛、灵活、顽强,布下锐阵等待交战,该怎样攻击呢?

答:攻击这样的敌军,我军必须分成三路兵

jointly counter-attack and achieve victory. This is the way to defeat the circular formation.

Q.: Given that the enemy is well stocked with provisions and is numerous and strong while we lack provisions and are few and weak, what should we do when he attacks us, using the square formation?

A.: Against such a formation, you need to set up a loose formation to compel the enemy to scatter his forces. Upon contact, feign withdrawal and defeat. Then turn around to attack him from behind his flanks. Remember, do not let him detect your intentions. This is the way to defeat the square formation.

Q.: Given that the enemy is numerous, strong, fierce, flexible and persistent, what should we do when he uses the sharp formation?

A.: Against such a formation, you divide your forces into three detachments to make the en-

【原文】

者延而衡,二者□□□□恐而下惑,上下既乱,三军大北。此击锐之道也。

交和而舍,敌既众以强,延阵以衡,我阵而待之,人少不能,击之奈何？击此者,必将三分我兵,练我死士,二者延阵张翼,一者材士练兵,期其中极。此杀将击衡之道也。

【今译】

马,以调动分散敌军。一路展开横队队形,其它两路攻击敌军侧后,使敌将帅惊惧,士卒惶恐,上下混乱一片,敌军必然大败。这就是击破锐阵的方法。

问：两军对阵,敌军既多又强,正面展开兵力布下横阵,我军也列阵待战,但兵少不能与敌对抗该怎样攻击它呢？

答：攻击这样的敌军,我军必须分兵三部分,精选武艺高强的敢死士卒,以两部分兵力摆开阵势分为两翼以掩护,一部分敢死的勇士打击敌人的要害部位,从中军之指挥所突破。这就是杀敌将帅、击破敌军横阵的方法。

emy scatter his forces. Use one detachment to set up a horizontal formation and send the other two detachments to attack him from behind his flanks. This move will alarm the enemy commander and frighten his soldiers. Once the enemy is seized with fear and confusion, he will end up in a rout. This is the way to defeat the sharp formation.

Q.: Given that the enemy is numerous and strong while we are few and are no match for him in strength, how should we attack him when confronted with the horizontal formation?

A.: Against such a formation, you may divide your forces to form three detachments. With two detachments to protect your flanks, your crack troops will attack the enemy command post in the center and effect a breakthrough. This is the way to kill the enemy commander and generals and crush his horizontal formation.

【原文】

交和而舍，我人兵则众，车骑则少，敌人十倍，击之奈何？击此者，当保险带隘，慎避广易。故易则利车，险则利徒。此击车之道也。

交和而舍，我车骑则众，人兵则少，敌人十倍，击之奈何？击此者，慎避险阻，决而导之，抵诸易。敌虽十倍，便我车骑，三军可击。此击徒人之道也。

【今译】

问：两军对阵，我军兵卒多，战车、骑兵少，敌军的车骑兵十倍于我，该怎样攻打呢？

答：攻击这样的敌军，应当占据险要的地形，避开平坦开阔的地带。因为平坦开阔地形对敌军车、骑作战有利，险要的地形对我步兵有利。这是攻击敌优势战车、骑兵的办法。

问：两军对阵，我军战车、骑兵多，步卒少，敌军步卒十倍于我，该怎样攻击呢？

答：攻击这样的敌军要避开险要地形，引诱敌人到平坦地带决战。敌军步卒虽十倍于我，但平坦地带便于我车、骑兵发挥威力，仍可打败敌军。这是攻击敌步兵优势的方法。

Q. : Given that our forces are composed mostly of foot soldiers but inadequate as to chariots and cavalry, and outnumbered ten to one by the enemy in this respect, what should we do when the two sides confront each other?

A. : Against such an enemy, you should occupy a position, which is strategically located and difficult of access, avoiding open level ground. This is because the latter is favorable for the use of chariots and cavalry while the former is favorable for the use of foot soldiers. This is the way to defeat an enemy superior in chariots and cavalry.

Q. : Given that we are superior in chariots and cavalry while the enemy outnumbers us ten to one in foot soldiers, what should we do when the two sides confront each other?

A. : Against such an enemy, you should avoid regions strategically located and difficult of access and draw the enemy to open and level ground. Although his foot soldiers are ten times as numerous as yours, the terrain is favorable to the use of chariots and cavalry and to victory over your enemy. This is the way to attack an enemy superior in infantry.

【原文】

交和而舍，粮食不属，人兵不足恃，绝根而攻，敌人十倍，击之奈何？曰：击此者，敌人既□而守阻，我……反而害其虚。此击争□之道也。

交和而舍，敌将勇而难惧，兵强人众自固，三军之士皆勇而无虑，其将则威，其兵则武，而理强梁是，诸侯莫之或待。击之奈何？曰：击此者，告之不敢，示之不能，坐拙而待

【今译】

问：两军对垒，我军粮食接济不上，兵力兵器又供给不足，我军远离后方作战，敌十倍于我，该怎样攻击呢？

答：攻打这样的敌军，敌多而且凭险据守，我军应见机用计，乘敌之隙，攻其弱点。这是攻击"必争之地"的敌军方法。

问：两军对阵，敌军将领勇猛无畏，敌既多又强，军阵巩固，敌三军士卒斗志旺盛，无所顾虑，将领有威信，士卒英武，官吏强干，粮食充足，诸侯不敢与其对抗。该怎样攻打呢？

答：要攻打这样的敌军，先扬言我们不敢打，显示我们没有力量打，装着屈服的样子对待敌人，

Q.: Given that we are far away from our home base, and are short on grain, manpower and weapons, while the enemy outnumbers us ten to one, what should we do when the two sides confront each other?

A.: When tackling such an enemy, since he is numerous and commands advantageous terrain, you should... await your chances and attack where he is weak. This is the way to defeat the enemy in hotly contested regions.

Q.: Given that the enemy is numerous and strong, his formation firm and solid, his army militant and in high spirits, his generals fearless and highly respected, his officers efficient and his soldiers brave, and furthermore, his provisions ample — in short, the kind of enemy that no state dares to oppose — what should we do when we have to face such an army?

A.: Against such an army, first spread the word that you dare not fight, that you are in no position to test your strength against him. By pretending that you are ready to yield to his power, you

【原文】

之，以骄其意，以惰其志，使敌弗识，因击其不□，攻其不御，压其骀，攻疑。彼既贵既武，三军徙舍，前后不相睹，故中而击之，若有徙与。此击强众之道也。

交和而舍，敌人保山而带阻，我远则不接，近则无所，击之奈何？击此者，彼敛阻移□□□□□则危之，攻其所必救，使离其固，以揆其虑，施伏设

【今译】

使敌人志骄意满，斗志松懈，摸不清我意图，然后击其不意，攻其不备，攻其弱点，乘其不知所措之时发起攻击。敌军勇猛，但骄傲自恃，敌军行动必然前后不能照应，我军趁机拦腰截击，这是一种示弱欺敌的方法，是攻击强大之敌的方法。

问：两军对阵，敌军据山守险，我军远离敌阵不能与其交战，离近了又没有可依托的地形，这种情况该怎样攻打？

答：攻打这样的敌军，它既然凭险据守，……就设法使其感到守险也有危险，攻击敌军必须援救的地方，迫使其离开固守的阵地，判明敌军行动意图，设置伏兵和援军，乘其大军移动时攻击。这

270

make the enemy drunk with pride. Thus he relaxes his vigilance and becomes fuzzy about your true intentions. Then catch him unprepared and unawares. Seek out his weak points and attack, and he will be thrown into a quandary. His soldiers, however brave, will fall into disarray because they are conceited and arrogant, and you can strike at the enemy formation at its waist. This is the method of defeating a powerful enemy by deceptive means while expanding your own strength in the process.

Q.: Given that the enemy is entrenched on a mountain far from our position, and if we try to get near him we will be exposed because of the terrain, what should we do?

A.: Since the enemy is entrenched in a stronghold, confrontation with him calls for trying to make him feel jittery where he is situated. Attack the place where he feels he must rush to the rescue and thus compel him to leave his entrenched position. Find out about the intentions of his movements, lay a trap and prepare troops for ambush and reinforcement. Attack the enemy when he is in movement. This is the way to overpower

【原文】

援,击其移庶。此击保固之道也。

交和而舍,客主两阵,敌人形箕,计敌所愿,欲我陷覆,击之奈何? 击此者,渴者不饮,饥者不食,三分用其二,其于中极,彼既□□,材士练兵,击其两翼,□彼□喜□□三军大北,此击箕之道也。

七百一十九

【今译】

是攻击据山守险之敌的方法。

问:两军对阵,双方列阵相峙,敌军布下畚箕形阵势,敌军企图陷我军于覆灭的境地,这样的情况该怎么打?

答:攻打这样的敌人,渴者不饮,饥者不食,用三分之二的兵力全力攻击敌军阵地正中央,待敌之两翼向我合围时,再用三分之一精选出的、武艺高强的士卒,攻击其两翼,使敌误认我军已被其包围,正在欢喜之时而全军大败。这就是攻破敌人畚箕形阵势的方法。

an enemy who is entrenched on a mountain.

Q.: What should we do when the two sides confront each other and the enemy sets up a dustbin formation ready to annihilate our troops?

A.: When faced with such a formation, see to it that the thirsty among you shall not drink and the hungry shall not eat. Use two-thirds of your troops to concentrate an attack against the center of the enemy's position; when the enemy's flanks close in on you, use the other one-third, consisting of crack troops well versed in martial arts, to break up the two flanks. The enemy, thinking that he has encircled you, is overjoyed only to find that a rout awaits him. This is the way to deal with the enemy's dustbin formation.

略　甲

略甲

　　　略甲之法,敌之人方阵□□无……

……欲击之,其势不可,夫若此者,下之……

……以国章,欲战若狂,夫若此者,少阵……

……反,夫若此者,以众卒从之,篡卒因之,必将……

……篡卒因之,必……

* * *

……左右旁伐以相趋,此谓镂钩击。

……之气不藏于心,三军之众□循之知不……

……将分□军以脩□□□□寡而民……

……威□□其难将之□也。分其众,乱其……

……阵不厉,故列不……

……远揄之,敌倦以远……

……治,孤其将,荡其心,击……

……其将勇,其卒众……

……彼大众将之……

……卒之道……

【编者按】

　　本篇简文残缺过多,无法释译成现代汉语和英语。谨存残简。

　　竹简整理小组注曰:"本篇字体与《十阵》、《十问》相近,不易区分,现将可能属于这三篇的残简一并附于本篇之后。"本书校释者认为,从本篇篇题看,似是打击强敌之意。

274

Dealing Blows at Enemy's
Crack Troops

Editors' Note: Too many characters are missing for us to make sense of what the text means and translate it into modern Chinese. The restoration team has given it the following annotation: "The calligraphic style on the strips is similar to that of 'Ten Formations' and 'Ten Questions on Warfare.' It has therefore been placed alongside these two chapters." We think it may have dealt with the topic of striking at a powerful enemy.

客主人分

客主人分

兵有客之分,有主人之分。客之分众,主人之分少。客倍主人半,然可敌也。

负……定者也。客者,后定者也。主人安地抚势以胥。夫客犯隘逾险而至,夫犯隘……退敢刎颈,进不敢拒敌,其故何也?势不

【今译】

用兵作战有客军和主军之分。进攻的客军兵力要多,防御的主军兵力可少。客军兵力是主军兵力的两倍,主军兵力是客军的一半,这样的力量对比也就可以对阵交锋了。

主军的阵势先定,客军的阵势后定。主军占据有利地形,严阵以待。客军则要越过关隘险阻才能到达战地。客军突破隘塞进入敌境后,有时宁愿冒杀头的危险后退,也不敢向前与敌交战,这是什么原因呢?〔这是因

Difference Between Guest and Host Armies

In war, there is a difference between guest and host armies. The invading guest army is usually more numerous than the invaded host army. When the host army is half the size of the guest army, then the balance of forces enables the former to engage the latter in battle.

... the host army takes up its position before the guest army. It occupies a favorable terrain and in full battle array awaits its enemy. The guest army, on the other hand, has to cross narrow passes and overcome other obstacles before it can reach the battleground. Why is it that sometimes the troops of the guest army, having broken through passes to enter enemy territory, would rather retreat and risk being executed than to move forward to fight the enemy? This is be-

【原文】

便,地不利也。势便地利则民自……自退。所谓善战者,便势利地者也。

带甲数十万,民有余粮弗得食也,有余……居兵多而用兵少也,居者有余而用者不足。

带甲数十万,千千而出,千千而□之……万万以遗我。所谓善战者,善蒿断之,如□会挠者也。能分人之兵,能按人之兵,则锱〔铢

【今译】

为〕形势与地形对客军不利。如果形势、地势对客军有利,士卒自然敢于前进。反之,就会自行败退。所谓善于指挥作战的人,在于因势利导,能够利用有利地形。

军队数十万,民有余粮也供养不起。……养兵的时候多,用兵的时候少;平时养兵感到太多,战时用兵就感到太少了。

军队数十万,成千成千地出征,成千成千地列阵,……而敌军可能成万成万地向我进攻。

所以善于指挥作战的人,要善于分割截断敌军,就像宰割牛羊那样。能分散、牵制敌军的兵力,就是兵少也有余;不能分散、牵制

cause both the situation andterrain are unfavorable to them. Should the situation and the terrain be favorable, the troops will continue their advance; otherwise they will retreat.... That is why a commander who knows how to take advantage of a situation and make good use of terrain is considered to be skilled in warfare.

When you have hundreds of thousands of troops under your command, the populace will be hard up even if they have surplus grain. An army is always too large to maintain but too small when you need to put them to use. During peacetime, you find you have maintained too large an army; but during war you find you don't have enough troops.

With an armed force hundreds of thousands strong, thousands upon thousands are sent on expeditions, thousands upon thousands are placed in formations... but tens of thousands of enemy troops may come and attack you, horde upon horde. He who is a capable commander knows how to intercept and tear up the enemy just as he would carve up a cow or a sheep. He who knows how to scatter and pin down the enemy effectives will find his own troops sufficient even if they

【原文】

而有余。不能分人之兵，不能按人之兵，则数倍而不足。众者胜乎？则投算而战耳。富者胜乎？则量粟而战耳。兵利甲坚者胜乎？则胜易知矣。故富未居安也，贫未居危也；众未居胜也，少〔未居败也〕。以决胜败安危者，道也。敌人众，能使之分离而不相救也，受敌者不得相……以为固，甲坚兵利不得以为强，士

【今译】

敌军兵力，就是兵力数倍于敌也感到不足。兵多就能取胜吗？那么只要计算一下兵力多少就可以战了；富足就能取胜吗？那么只要量一量粮食多少就可以战了；武器装备精良就能取胜吗？那胜利也就太容易未战先知了。所以，国家富足未必安全，国家贫困不一定危险；兵多未必胜利，兵少〔不一定失败〕。决定胜败安危的，在于能否掌握用兵打仗的道理。敌军众多，能使其分离而不能相互求援；受到攻击而不知情；深沟高垒不能用以固守；装备备精良不能发挥威力；士卒勇猛而不能

are few. He who does not will find his troops insufficient even if they outnumber the enemy many times over.

If victory could be assured when your troops outnumber the enemy's, then all you would have to do is to count the number of troops on both sides. If victory could be assured when you are prosperous and your grain supply surpasses the enemy's, then it would be enough simply to measure how much grain the two sides have to predict which side will be victorious. If victory could be assured when you have better weapons and equipment than the enemy, then it would be only too easy to forecast victory. Therefore, prosperity does not necessarily guarantee a nation's security and poverty does not necessarily mean a nation will be in peril. Superiority in the number of troops does not necessarily signify victory, and inferiority in number does. Victory or defeat, security or peril, what is decisive is whether you have mastered the art of war. Against an enemy superior in number, it is possible to divide it into pockets so that they are unable to help each other. Furthermore, it is possible to make the well-armed troops unable to fully display their

【原文】

有勇力不得以卫其将，则胜有道矣。

故明主、知道之将必先□，可有功于未战之前，故不失；可有之功于已战之后。故兵出而有功，入而不伤，则明于兵者也。

五百一十四

* * *

……焉。为人客则先人作……

……兵曰：主人逆客于境……

……客好事则……

……使劳，三军之士可使毕失其志，则胜

【今译】

保卫其将帅。这就掌握取胜的道理了。

所以，英明的君主，懂得用兵打仗的将帅，必须战前〔周密谋划，做好战争准备〕，这样，战前就有了胜利的把握，开战以后就会赢得胜利。所以出兵就能获得胜利，退兵也不会受损。这才是善于用兵的人。

* * *

……让敌人疲惫，使敌全军将士丧失斗

power, to make the courageous and fierce soldiers unable to protect their generals. When you have done all that, then it can be said that you have acquired the secrets to victory.

Hence, the wise sovereign and commander who know the art of war must plan carefully and make full preparations before they go to war. In this way, they have the assurances of victory prior to the war and they will win after it breaks out; they are sure of victory when they go to battle and they will not suffer losses when they withdraw. These are the people who are truly adept at warfare. . . .

* * *

. . . Once you have exhausted the enemy and demoralized his generals and soldiers, then you

【原文】

可得而据也。是以按左抶右，右败而左弗能救；按右抶左，左败而右弗能救。是以兵坐而不起，避而不用，近者少而不足用，远者疏而不能……

【今译】

志，取得胜利就有把握了。所以牵制敌军的左翼，打击其右翼，使其右翼失败，左翼不能援救；牵制敌人的右翼，打击其左翼，使其左翼失败，右翼不能援救。使敌人军队动弹不得，避而不战，近处的兵力少了不够用，远处的被分散而不能〔救援〕……

are sure of victory. You can attack his right flank while tying down his left flank so that it cannot come to the former's rescue, and vice versa. Then the enemy will find that his troops have been immobilized and cannot fight a battle, that he has few troops close by to meet his needs and his other forces have been distanced far away, rendering them useless to him...

善 者

【原文】

善者

　　善者,敌人军□人众,能使分离而不相救也,受敌而不相知也。故沟深垒高不得以为固,车坚兵利不得以为威,士有勇力而不得以为强。故善者制险量阻,敦三军,利屈伸,敌人众能使寡,积粮盈军能使饥,安处不动能使

【今译】

　　善于用兵的人,能使兵强人众的敌军兵力分散而不能互相救援;能使其受到攻击彼此还不知情况。因此,敌军构筑深沟高垒也不能用来固守,敌装备精良也不能发挥威力,士卒勇猛也不能用来表现强悍。因此,善于用兵的人能够审度地形,利用险阻,屯驻三军,进退自如。敌军虽多,使其感到兵力不足;粮食虽充足,能使其挨饿;安处不动,能使

He Who Is Adept
at Warfare

He who is adept at warfare can not only make a powerful and massive enemy scatter his forces but also prevent them from helping each other. He can place them under attack without their knowing what is happening to the other ranks. Hence, the enemy who is entrenched behind deep gullies and high ramparts is unable to defend himself; the enemy who is well equipped is unable to display his strength; and his soldiers, courageous as they may be, are unable to demonstrate their prowess.

He who is adept at warfare knows how to make use of the terrain and take advantage of the dangerous and difficult passes to facilitate his troops' advance and retreat. He knows how to make the enemy commander feel hard pressed for lack of man power even though he may be in command of a large force. He knows how to make an enemy, even with ample provisions, suffer from hunger. He knows how to wear out his adversaries even

【原文】

劳,得天下能使离,三军和能使柴。

　　故兵有四路、五动:进,路也;退,路也;左,路也;右,路也。进,动也;退,动也;左,动也;右,动也;默然而处,亦动也。善者四路必彻,五动必工。故进不可迎于前,退不可绝于后。左右不可陷于阻,默〔然而处〕,□□于敌之人。

【今译】

其疲劳;得到民众能使其失去民众;三军同心,能使其不和产生怨恨。

　　军队作战有"四路"、"五动"。四路是:进路,退路,左路,右路。五动有:前进,后退,向左,向右,按兵不动也是动。善于用兵的人能使"四路"通达、"五动"自如。进攻时,敌军不能阻挡,撤退时,敌军不能截断退路,左、右行动时不会受阻,按兵不动时也会威震敌人。

though they may stay put. He knows how to create discontent among the contented enemy populace and how to create dissension among united enemy troops.

For an army, there are "four routes" and "five kinds of movement." The "four routes" are: forward, backward, to the left and to the right. The "five kinds of movement" are: advance, retreat, left turn, right turn and staying in place, for even that is a kind of movement. He who is adept at warfare sees to it that his "four routes" are open and any of the "five kinds of movement" can be adopted at will. When he attacks, the enemy knows not how to stop him. When he retreats, the enemy knows not how to block him. When he heads left or right, he can move unhindered. Even when he stays put, he remains a threat to the enemy.

【原文】

故使敌四路必穷,五动必忧。进则傅于前,退则绝于后,左右则陷于阻,默然而处,军不免于患。善者能使敌卷甲趋远,倍道兼行,倦病而不得息,饥渴而不得食。以此薄敌,战必不胜矣。我饱食而待其饥也,安处以待其劳也,正静以待其动也。故民见进而不见退,蹈白刃而不还踵。

二百□□□

【今译】

对于敌军要使其"四路"受阻、"五动"不利。进攻时受到阻击,撤退时后路被截断,左右行动时受到牵制,按兵不动时也难免遭受打击。

善于用兵的人,能够调动敌军卷起铠甲长途跋涉,昼夜兼程,疲于奔命,疲惫而得不到休息,饥渴得不到饮食。用这种方法消耗敌军,敌军必败无疑矣。而我军以饱待饥,以逸待劳,以严整镇静待动乱之敌。这样,我军与敌交战时就会勇敢向前,绝不后退,踏着锋刃也不会调头溃逃。

On the other hand, it is necessary for him to block his enemy's "four routes" and to make it difficult for him to employ any of the "five kinds of movement". The enemy is blocked when he attacks, intercepted when he withdraws, and checked whether he moves left or right. Even when he remains where he is, he still cannot avert constant blows.

He who is adept at war can make the enemy carry heavy amour and march long distances day and night until he is completely tired out but without a chance to rest, hungry and thirsty but without food and water. Thus, using the method of weakening the enemy by attrition, he makes certain that his foe is doomed to failure. His own army, on the other hand, can await a hungry enemy with well-fed troops, await a fatigued enemy with well-rested troops and await an alarmed enemy with perfect calm. In this way, when his troops engage the enemy, they will fight courageously, keep advancing and never turn back or run away even if it means "walking on knife-edge"!

五名五恭

【原文】

兵有五名:一曰威强,二曰轩骄,三曰刚
至,四曰肋忌,五曰重柔。夫威强之兵,则屈软
而待之;轩骄之兵,则恭敬而久之;刚至之
兵,则诱而取之;肋忌之兵,则薄其前,谍其
旁,深沟高垒而难其粮;重柔之兵,则谍而恐

【今译】

敌军分为五种类型:一是威武顽强,二是
高傲骄横,三是刚愎自用,四是胆小多疑,五是
优柔寡断。对于威武顽强的敌军,用示弱的办
法对待它;对于高傲骄横的敌军,故作恭敬,伺
机消灭它;对于刚愎自用的敌军,用引诱的
办法战胜它;对于胆小多疑的敌军,威迫其正
面,袭扰其两翼,构筑深沟高垒断其粮道;
对于优柔寡断的敌军,用鼓噪的办法恐吓

Five Types of Army

There are five types of army: 1) powerful and tenacious, 2) arrogant and imperious, 3) headstrong and self-willed, 4) timid and suspicious, and 5) weak and hesitant.

When up against a powerful and tenacious enemy, appear to be weak and await your chance. When faced by the arrogant and imperious, appear to be respectful and find an opportunity to eliminate him. When tacking the headstrong and self-willed, overcome him by inducement. When handling the timid and suspicious, threaten his front, harass his flanks and cut off his supply line by digging deep gullies and building high ramparts. When tackling a weak and hesitant enemy, frighten him with an uproar, disturb him with

【原文】

之,振而捅之,出则击之,不出则回之。

五名

兵有五恭、五暴。何谓五恭？入境而恭,军失其常。再举而恭,军无所粮。三举而恭,军失其事。四举而恭,军无食。五举而恭,军不及事。入境而暴,谓之客。再举而暴,谓之

【今译】

它,用袭击的办法触动它,出来就打,不出来则围困它。

进入敌境的军队往往有五恭(五种宽柔表现),五暴(五种威慑暴虐行为)。什么叫五恭？一入敌境即宽柔,军队就会失去应有的威严。再次宽柔,军队就会征集不到粮草。三次宽柔,军队就会贻误战机。四次宽柔,军队就会断炊。五次宽柔,军队就无法完成任务。什么叫五暴？一入敌境就采取威慑暴烈众行动,敌国民会当作外寇。二次施暴,会被

probes, set on him should he ever dare come out and encircle him if he doesn't.

When an army enters enemy territory, it often carries out policies which might be described as "five gentlenesses and leniencies" and "five harshnesses and coercions."

What do we mean by the "five gentlenesses and leniencies?" The army which is gentle and lenient as soon as it enters enemy territory will lose dignity and prestige. The second time this happens, it will have difficulty collecting local provisions. The third time, it will miss its chances of winning a battle. The fourth, it will have to go without food. And the fifth, the army will not be able to accomplish its tasks.

The guest army which takes harsh and coercive actions immediately after it enters enemy territory will be looked upon by the local people as an invader. The second time it does so, it will be

【原文】

华。三举而暴，主人惧。四举而暴，卒士见诈。
五举而暴，兵必大耗。故五恭、五暴，必使相错
也。

五恭

二百五十六

【今译】

当作邪恶军队。第三次施暴，敌国民众就会恐
惧。第四次施暴，军队就会得不到真实情报。
第五次施暴，军队就会受到很大的损失。所以
恭、暴必须交替并举。

considered an evil force. The third time, the local people will be terrified. The fourth, it will not be able to secure any reliable information. And the fifth, the army will suffer great losses. Hence, it is absolutely necessary to combine gentleness with harshness, leniency with coercion, alternating between one and the other as the case demands.

〔兵　失〕

【原文】

欲以敌国之民之所不安,正俗所……难敌国兵之所长,耗兵也。欲强多国之所寡,以应敌国之所多,速屈之兵也。

备固,不能难敌之器用,陵兵也。器用不利,敌之备固,挫兵也。

【今译】

欲想用敌国民众所不能接受的东西去纠正那个国家的习俗,想勉强以自己的短处去对付敌国军队的长处,会白白地损耗兵力。想勉强增加自己国家所缺少的,去对付敌国所多的,就会加快军队的失败。

防御设施不能抵御敌人的进攻器械,军队就会受到压制。进攻的武器装备不精良,不能攻破敌军的坚固防御设施,军队就会遭到挫败。

Losses in Battle

He who hopes to change the customs of the enemy country by forcing on its populace what is unacceptable to them is countering the enemy's advantages with his own disadvantages and is merely wasting his own time and effort. He who strains his efforts to increase what he lacks to counter what the enemy abounds in will only accelerate his own defeat.

When the defense installations cannot cope with the enemy's offensive weapons, the troops will feel depressed. When their own offensive weapons are defective and cannot break through the enemy's defense installations, the troops will feel frustrated.

【原文】

兵不……明者也。善阵,知背向,知地形,而兵数困,不明于国胜、兵胜者也。

民……兵不能昌大功,不知会者也。兵失民,不知过者也。兵用力多功少,不知时者也。兵不能胜大患,不能合民心者也。兵多悔,信疑者也。兵不能见福祸于未形,不知备者也。

【今译】

军队不〔能取胜〕,是将帅不懂得行军布阵与征伐时所向或所背的原故。善于布阵,懂得布阵的背向,也善于利用地形,而军队却往往陷入困境,那是由于不懂得战略上的胜利与战场上胜利的关系。

民众支持的军队而不能创建战功,那是不善于集中兵力作战的原故。军队得不到民众的支持,那是由于不知道自己的过错所在。军队征战多战功少,是由于没有抓住有利的战机。军队不能战胜强敌,是由于不符合民众的心愿。军队动摇,是由于听信谣言。军队不能预见作战的胜败,是由于不知道做好战前各种准备的原故。

An army cannot win when the commander does not understand how to set up formations and how to direct his troops on the march. When the commander is good at setting up formations and knows the direction they should follow and is familiar with the lay of the land, and yet his army is trapped in a difficult situation, that is because he doesn't understand the relationship between strategic victory and victory on the battlefield.

Sometimes an army has the support of the populace and still fails to achieve great victory; that is because it does not know how to concentrate its forces. Failure of an army to gain the support of the populace results from failure to realize where it is in the wrong. When an army has fought many battles but achieved few victories, it is because it does not know how to seize the opportunity for victory. When an army fails to win victory over a powerful enemy, it is because it has gone against the will of the populace. An army's will is shaken if it is beset with rumors. An army can have no idea of the outcome of a battle if it has not made all the necessary preparations beforehand.

【原文】

兵见善而怠，时至而疑，去非而弗能居，止道也。

贪而廉，龙而敬，弱而强，柔而〔刚〕，起道也。

行止道者，天地弗能兴也。行起道者，天地……

* * *

……之兵也。欲以国……

……内疲之兵也。多费不固……

……见敌难服。兵尚淫天地……

……而兵强国……

……兵不能……

【今译】

军队遇到有利条件不能及时利用，面临有利战机却犹豫不决，认识到指挥错误，但不能实施正确指挥，这是灭亡之道。

贪婪的人能变廉洁，骄傲的人能变谨慎，怯弱的人能变坚定，软弱的人能变刚强，是兴旺之道。行灭亡之道，天地不能使其兴旺。行兴旺之道，天地也不能使其衰败。……

An army will end in ruin if it hesitates when favored with excellent conditions, if it does not know how to make timely use of its opportunities and if it realizes its mistakes but does not know how to act correctly.

The avaricious can become upright, the proud become careful, the timid become firm, and the weak become strong. That is the way to the army's enhancement.

He who persists in the way of ruin, neither heaven nor earth can help him flourish. He who follows the way of enhancement, neither heaven nor earth can lead him to ruin.

将　义

【原文】

义将

　　将者不可以不义,不义则不严,不严则不威,不威则卒弗死。故义者,兵之首也。

　　将者不可以不仁,不仁则军不克,军不克则军无功。故仁者,兵之腹也。

　　将者不可以无德,无德则无力,无力则三

【今译】

　　作为将帅不可以不义,不义则不严明,不严明则没有威信,没有威信士卒则不肯效命。所以,将帅的"义"就像军队的头部一样。

　　作为将帅不可以不仁,不仁则军队就不能克敌制胜,不能克敌制胜也就不能建立战功。因此,"仁"就像军队的腹部一样。

　　作为将帅不可以无德,无德则指挥无力,

The Commander's Righteousness

It is essential for a commander to be righteous. If he is not righteous, he cannot be strict; if he is not strict, he cannot command respect; if he cannot command respect, his soldiers will not fight and sacrifice for the cause. Therefore, the commander's righteousness is like the brain of the army.

It is essential for a commander to be benevolent. If he is not benevolent, his army cannot overpower the enemy; if it cannot overpower the enemy, it cannot be successful in battle. Therefore, the commander's benevolence is like the abdomen of the army.

It is essential for a commander to be virtuous. If he is not virtuous, his orders will not carry weight, and without orders that carry weight to

【原文】

军之利不得。故德者,兵之手也。

将者不可以不信,不信则令不行,令不行则军不桡,军不桡则无名。故信者,兵之足也。

将者不可以不智胜,不智胜……则军无□。故决者,兵之尾也。

将义

【今译】

指挥无力则三军不能取得胜利。所以"德"就像军队的双手一样。

作为将帅不可以不讲信用,无信用军令则不能贯彻执行,军令不能贯彻执行,军队则不能统一指挥。军队不能统一指挥则不能成功成名。所以,"信"就像军队的双足一样。

作为将帅不可以不预知胜负,不预知胜负,指挥就不能〔果断,指挥不果断〕,……所以,果断,就像军队的尾翼一样。

direct the army, it will not be able to score victories. Therefore, the commander's virtues are like the hands of the army.

It is essential for a commander to be trustworthy. If he cannot be trusted, his orders will not be carried out; and when they cannot be carried out, the army will not have a unified command. When that is the case, it will have no hope of success and fame. Therefore, the commander's trustworthiness is like the feet of the army.

A commander must be able to predict the outcome of a battle. If he doesn't know what will happen, he cannot direct the battle with resolve.... Therefore, the commander's resolution is like the tail and wings of the army.

〔将　德〕

【原文】

……赤子,爱之若狡童,敬之若严师,用之若土芥,将军……

……不失,将军之智也,不轻寡,不劫于敌,慎终若始,将军……

……而不御,君令不入军门,将军之恒

【今译】

……将帅看待士卒要像看待单纯的孩子一样,爱护士卒要像爱护娇好的幼童一样,敬重士卒要像敬重尊严的老师一样,使用士卒要像泥土草芥一样,毫不吝惜。

……将帅之明智在于不轻视弱小敌军,不惧怕强敌威胁,身为将帅自始至终,慎重从事。……

……将帅在指挥作战上不应受君主的牵制,将在外君不御将之意,〔这是将帅应坚持

Virtues in a Commander

The commander treats his soldiers as if they were little children and loves them as if they were his own offspring. He respects them as if they were his teachers. But when he uses them, he does so without the least compunction as if they were no more than mud and grass. . . .

The wisdom of the commander lies in this: he does not belittle the most insignificant enemy, nor does he fear the most powerful enemy. He is prudent and cautious from beginning to end. . . .

The commander in the field will not allow interference in his command. This is a principle he

【原文】

也。入军……

……将不两生，军不两存，将军之……

……将军之惠也。赏不逾日，罚不还面，不维其人，不何外辰，此将军之德也。

【今译】

的原则〕。……

……〔三军与敌交战时〕，将帅不与敌将共生，军队不与敌军共存。……

……将帅的恩惠在于对有功者立即奖赏，有过者立刻惩罚，不分亲疏贵贱，不受外来的权威所干预。这是将军应具备的品德。

must stick to. . . : [When in battle], the commander will not allow himself to coexist with the commander of the enemy forces, nor his troops with their counterparts. . . .

The benevolence of the commander is manifested in the rewards he offers to those who have rendered meritorious services, and the punishment he promptly metes out to those who have committed mistakes. It matters not whether they are close or distant to him, and whether their posts are high or low. When performing his duties, he refuses to accept any interference from higher authorities. This is an essential quality in a capable commander.

将　败

【原文】

将败

　　将败：一曰不能而自能。二曰骄。三曰贪于位。四曰贪于财。〔五曰〕□。六曰轻。七曰迟。八曰寡勇。九曰勇而弱。十曰寡信。十一〔曰〕……十四曰寡决。十五曰缓。

【今译】

　　将帅致败的原因：一是无能而妄自逞能。二是骄傲自大。三是贪图名位。四是贪图钱财。五是……。六是轻率行动。七是迟钝。八是缺乏勇气。九是勇而无智。十是缺少信用。十一是……。十四是优柔寡断。十五是

Failings in a Commander

There are many failings which cause a commander to suffer defeat.

1) He thinks highly of himself when in fact he is incompetent.

2) He is conceited.

3) He is after fame and position.

4) He is after money and riches.

5) ...

6) He is reckless.

7) He is dull and slow.

8) He lacks courage.

9) He is courageous but lacks wisdom.

10) ... He is not trustworthy.

11) ...

12) ...

13) ...

14) He is irresolute and vacillating.

【原文】

十六曰怠。十七曰□。十八曰贼。十九曰自私。廿曰自乱。多败者多失。

【今译】

军纪松弛。十六是疏忽懈怠。十七是……。十八是残暴。

十九是自私。二十是指挥不利，自己造成部队混乱。将帅缺陷愈多，作战失败越多。

15) He is lax in enforcing discipline.

16) He is careless and lazy.

17) . . .

18) He is cruel.

19) He is selfish.

20) His command is remiss and inconsistent; so that his officers and soldiers are confused.

The more the commander's failings, the more frequent his defeats.

〔将　失〕

A
Moorish Collection of Scattered laos
(b) He is lax in enforcing discipline.
(c) He is careless and easy.
(d) He is timid.
(e) He is rash.
(f) He is slow.
20. His command is confused and inconsistent, so that his officers and soldiers are confused.
The more the commander's failings

【原文】

　　将失：一曰，失所以往来，可败也。二曰，收乱民而还用之，止北卒而还斗之，无资而有资，可败也。三曰，是非争，谋事辩讼，可败也。四曰，令不行，从不壹，可败也。五曰，下不服，众不为用，可败也。六曰，民苦其师，可败也。七曰，师老，可败也。八曰，师怀，可败

【今译】

　　将帅战败的原因有以下各种：一、军队往来调动失当，可导致失败。二、收集乱民、败卒参战，本无实力而自以为有实力，可导致失败。三、是非辩论不决，谋事争执不决，可导致失败。四、军令不能贯彻执行，军队行动不统一，可导致失败。五、下级不服从上级，士卒不愿效力，可导致失败。六、民众痛恨军队，可导致失败。七、军队长期出征在外，疲惫不堪，士气低落，可导致失败。八、士卒怀念家乡，可导致失败。

Reasons for a
Commander's Defeat

For the following reasons, a commander may suffer defeat:

1) Wrong movements of troops.

2) Absorbing worthless people and defeated soldiers into his ranks..., with the mistaken notion that this will increase his strength.

3) Protracted dispute over right and wrong and endless discussion about matters of importance.

4) Lack of unity of action resulting from his inability to enforce orders.

5) Disobedience among the ranks and unwillingness on their part to serve the country.

6) Popular hatred for the troops.

7) General war fatigue and low morale among the soldiers as a result of prolonged service.

8) The spread of homesickness among the soldiers.

【原文】

也。九曰,兵遁,可败也。十曰,兵□不□,可败也。十一曰,军数惊,可败也。十二曰,兵道足陷,众苦,可败也。十三曰,军事险固,众劳,可败也。十四〔曰〕,□□□备,可败也。十五曰,日暮路远,众有至气,可败也。十六曰,……可败也。十七〔曰〕,……众恐,可败也。十八曰,令数变,众偷,可败也。十九曰,军淮,众不能其将吏,可败也。廿曰,多幸,众怠,可败也。廿一曰,多疑,众疑,可败也。廿二曰,恶闻其过,可败

【今译】

九、士卒逃亡,可导致失败。十、军队内部不〔团结〕,可导致失败。十一、军队屡遭惊扰,可导致失败。十二、行军路途泥泞,士卒劳苦,可遭失败。十三、军队构筑坚固工事要塞,士卒劳累过度,可导致失败。十四、军队〔疏于戒备〕,可导致失败。十五、日暮途远,士卒埋怨,可导致失败。十六、……。十七、……。十八、军令反复更改,士卒敷衍塞责,可导致失败。十九、军心涣散,士卒不尊重将吏,可导致失败。二十、将帅多偏爱,士卒懈怠,可导致失败。二十一、将帅犹豫不决,士卒无所适从,可导致失败。二十二、将帅厌恶

9) Mass desertion.

10) Disunity within the army.

11) Repeated shocks and disturbances, too much for the troops to bear.

12) Troops bogged down by muddy roads.

13) Troops exhausted by overwork during construction of fortifications and fortresses.

14) [Lack of] vigilance on the part of the troops.

15) Low morale of the troops who find at the end of the day that they still have a long way to go.

16) ...

17) ...

18) Indifference among the rank and file caused by repeated contradictory orders.

19) Sagging morale and the soldiers' disrespect for their superiors.

20) Partiality on the part of the commander causing sluggishness among the troops.

21) Indecision on the part of the commander causing confusion among the rank and file.

22) The commander's dislike of anyone who

【原文】

也。廿三曰，与不能，可败也。廿四曰，暴露伤志，可败也。廿五曰，期战心分，可败也。廿六曰，恃人之伤气，可败也。廿七曰，事伤人，恃伏诈，可败也。廿八曰，军舆无□，〔可败也。廿九曰，〕□下卒，众之心恶，可败也。卅曰，不能以成阵，出于夹道，可败也。卅一曰，兵之前行后行之兵，不参齐于阵前，可败也。卅二曰，战而忧前者

【今译】

别人指出其过失，可导致失败。二十三、任用无能的人，可导致失败。二十四、军队长期在国外作战，士气挫伤，可导致失败。二十五、约期交战军心涣散，可导致失败。二十六、指望敌军丧失斗志，存侥幸取胜心理，可导致失败。二十七、将帅仅仅指望敌人士气低落，单纯依靠阴谋诡计，可导致失败。二十八、……。二十九、将帅刻薄士卒，士卒心怀憎恨，可导致失败。三十、军队没有列成阵势，通过狭谷隘道，可导致失败。三十一、军队前行和后行的兵器，不能取长补短、相互配合，在阵前发挥威力，可导致失败。三十二、作

dares to point out his faults to him.

23) The commander appointing incapable officers.

24) The sagging morale of the rank and file because of prolonged battles and absence from
home.

25) Low morale caused by fear of impending
battle.

26) The commander leaving things to chance
and banking on the enemy's low morale.

27) The commander pinning his hopes on a
weakened enemy or relying wholly on schemes
and intrigues to gain victory.

28) ...

29) Extreme hatred on the part of the soldiers
for the commander, who treats them with dis-
dain.

30) The army marching along narrow paths
without a solid formation.

31) Lack of order in the formation, causing
poor coordination between the front and the rear,
with the result that the different contingents cannot play their full roles.

32) Lack of coordination during battle so that

【原文】

后虚,忧后者前虚,忧左者右虚,忧右者左虚。战而有忧,可败也。

【今译】

战时忧虑前面,后面空虚;忧虑后面,前面空虚;忧虑左面,右面空虚;忧虑右面,左面空虚。忧虑重重,顾此失彼,可导致失败。

the rear becomes weak when the front is strong and the left flank becomes weak while the right flank is strong, and vice versa. Defeat awaits those who are beset with worries and who have too many things to look after at the same time.

〔雄牝城〕

【原文】

城在淠泽之中,无亢山名谷,而有付丘于其四方者,雄城也,不可攻也。军食流水,〔生水也,不可攻〕也。城前名谷,背亢山,雄城也,不可攻也。城中高外下者,雄城也,不可攻也。城中有付丘者,雄城也,不可攻也。

【今译】

城地处在低洼沼泽地带,虽无高山屏障深谷为堑,但四面有连绵丘陵为依托,这是难攻的城,不可攻打。敌军喝的是流动的水,〔水源充足,这是难攻的城不可攻打〕。城前临深谷,背靠高山,这是难攻的城,不可攻打。城建在高处,城外四周地势低,这是难攻的城,不可攻打。城内起伏连绵的土丘,这是难攻的城,不可攻打。

Male and Female Cities

Some cities do not have mountains as bulwarks or deep valleys as moats but they have rolling hills all around them. These cities are known as male cities, which are difficult to attack and should not be attacked. Similarly, an army which is supplied with running water to drink [should not be besieged]. The same holds true for a city, with deep valleys in the front and mountains in the back, a city built on high land with low land all around it, or a city situated on rolling hills.

【原文】

营军趣舍，毋回名水，伤气弱志，可击也。城背名谷，无亢山其左右，虚城也，可击也。□尽烧者，死壤也，可击也。军食泛水者，死水也，可击也。城在发泽中，无名谷付丘者，牝城也，可击也。城在亢山间，无名谷付丘者，牝城也，可击也。城前亢山，背名谷，前高后下者，牝城也，可击也。

【今译】

敌人在行军途中宿营，无大江大河环绕屏蔽，士气低落，军无斗志，可以进击。城倚背深谷，左右无高山屏障，这是易攻的城，可以攻打。〔城坐落在贫瘠不毛的土地上〕，可以攻打。军队饮用地面积水，水源不足，可以攻打。城坐落在大片沼泽地带，无深谷为堑，无连绵山丘为依托，这是易攻的城，可以攻打。城地处大山之间，无深谷为堑，也无连绵山丘为依托，这是易攻的城，可以攻打。城前临高山，背靠深谷，前高后低，这是易攻的城，可以攻打。

When an army, which is low in spirits and has little enthusiasm for fighting, encamps in an area without river for protection, it is easy prey. A city which has no mountain on either flank but only a deep valley behind it is a female city which is easy to seize and can be attacked. [A city] built on poor land may be attacked. An army which has to rely on stagnant water and is therefore without an adequate water supply is easy prey. A city which is surrounded by marshes but does not have rolling hills or mountains as a bulwark nor deep gullies to form a moat is a female and pregnable city. The same holds true for a city which is situated amidst mountains but has no deep gullies as a moat, nor rolling hills as a bulwark, or one which has mountains in the front and deep gullies in the back, in other words, high in the front and low in the back.

〔五度九夺〕

【原文】

……矣,救者至,又重败之。故兵之大数,五十里不相救也。况近□□□□□数百里,此程兵之极也。故兵曰:积弗如,勿与持久;众弗如,勿与接和。□〔弗如,勿与□□。□弗如,勿〕与□长。习弗如,毋当其所长。五度既明,兵乃横行。故兵……趋敌数,一曰

【今译】

……援兵救援,又遭重挫。所以用兵作战的原则是,五十里外就不能救援,更何况近在百余里,远在数百里以外呢? 五十里驰兵求援是最大限度。兵法说,物资储备不如敌方,不要与敌持久作战。兵力不如敌方,不要与敌正面对阵。……训练不如敌方,不要与敌之所长较量。掌握处置好这五种情况,军队就能行动自如。所以用兵作战要与敌抢先

Five Principles and
Nine Seizures

... When the reinforcements finally arrive,
they again meet with defeat.

Therefore, the principles of war affirm that reinforcements should not be sent to help friendly
forces in need when they are more than 50 *li*
away, and certainly not when they are several
hundred *li* away. The maximum distance for reinforcements is 50 *li*. *The Rules of War* stipulates:
Do not fight a protracted battle against an enemy
whose provisions are enough to outlast yours. Do
not fight a frontal battle against an enemy whose
troops outnumber yours.... Do not .... Do not
contend against the enemy's strong points when its
troops are better trained than yours.... When
you have mastered the above five principles, your
army will operate with ease.

【原文】

取粮。二曰取水。三曰取津。四曰取途。五曰取险。六曰取易。七曰〔取□。八曰取□。九〕曰取其所读贵。凡九夺,所以趋敌也。

四百二字

【今译】

夺取九个方面:第一,夺取粮食。第二,夺取水源。第三,夺取渡口。第四,夺取交通要道。第五,夺取险要地势。第六,夺取平原地带。第七,……。第八,……。第九,夺取敌军要害。以上九夺,都是克敌制胜的必要手段。

Thus, in battle, ... you must seize the following from the enemy: 1) Grain, 2) sources of water supply, 3) ferry points, 4) key lines of communication, 5) ground which is strategically important and difficult of access, 6) plains, 7) ..., 8) ... and 9) positions which are crucial to the enemy.

These are all required actions for vanquishing the enemy.

〔积 疏〕

【原文】

〔积〕胜疏,盈胜虚,径胜行,疾胜徐,从胜寡,佚胜劳。

积故积之,疏故疏之,盈故盈之,虚〔故虚之,径故径〕之,行故行之,疾故疾之,〔徐故徐之,众故众〕之,寡故寡之,佚故佚之,劳故劳之。

积疏相为变,盈虚〔相为变,径行相为〕变,疾徐相为变,众寡相〔为变,佚劳相〕为变。

【今译】

……〔兵力集中〕胜于分散,雄厚胜于虚弱,突然临敌胜于通常攻击,行动迅速胜于缓慢,兵多胜于兵少,安逸胜于疲劳。

兵力该集中就集中,该分散就分散,该实就实,该虚就虚,该突然就突然,该正常就正常,该快就快,〔该慢就慢,该多就多〕,该少就少,该休整就休整,该劳累就劳累。

军队集中与分散可以相互转变,实与弱〔可以相互转变〕,突然袭击与正常攻击可以

Concentration and Dispersion

... To concentrate is better than to disperse, to be strong is better than to be weak, to launch a sudden assault is better than to launch an expected attack, to move quickly is better than to move slowly, to have many troops is better than to have few troops, and to be rested is better than to be tired out.

Act as the situation requires: concentrate or disperse, be strong or be weak, launch a sudden attack or a normal, routine attack, be quick or [be slow, be numerous or be few], be rested or be tired.

Concentration and dispersion of troops are interchangeable, and one can evolve into the other. So are strength and weakness, sudden attack and normal attack, fast pace and slow pace, many

【原文】

毋以积当积，毋以疏当疏，毋以盈当盈，毋以虚当虚，毋以疾当疾，毋以徐当徐，毋以众当众，毋以寡当寡，毋以佚当佚，毋以劳当劳。

积疏相当，盈虚相〔当，径行相当，疾徐相当，众寡〕相当，佚劳相当。敌积故可疏，盈故可虚，径故可行，疾〔故可徐，众故可寡，佚故可劳〕。……

【今译】

相互转变，行动迅速和缓慢可以相互转变，多与少可以相互转变，安逸与疲劳可以相互转变。

不要以兵力集中对付集中，以分散对付分散，以实对实，以虚对虚，以快对快，以慢对慢，以兵力多对付兵力多，以兵力少对付兵力少，以安逸对付安逸，以疲劳对付疲劳。

军队集中和分散是相对的，实与虚是相对的，〔突然和正常是相对的，快和慢是相对的，多与少是相对的〕，安逸和疲劳是相对的。所以敌军兵力集中可以使其分散，敌军兵力充实可以使其虚弱，敌军猝然行动可以使其失去突然性，〔行动迅速可以使其迟缓，安逸可以使其疲劳〕。……

and few, and being rested and being tired.

Do not meet concentration with concentration, dispersion with dispersion, strength with strength, weakness with weakness, fast pace with fast pace, slow pace with slow pace, many with many, few with few, restfulness with restfulness, and tiredness with tiredness.

Concentration and dispersion are relative, and so are the other pairs.

Therefore, you can turn the enemy's concentrated troops into dispersed ones; a strong enemy into a weak enemy; make the enemy's sudden assault lose its suddenness; [slowdown the enemy's speedy action and make the rested enemy tired].

奇　正

【原文】

奇正

　　天地之理，至则反，盈则败，□□是也；代兴代废，四时是也；有胜有不胜，五行是也；有生有死，万物是也；有能有不能，万生是也；有所有余，有所不足，形势是也。

　　故有形之徒，莫不可名。有名之徒，莫不

【今译】

　　天地间的事物，物极必反，盛极必衰，这是事物发展的必然规律；兴废更替，春夏秋冬也是这样循环更替；一种事物制胜另一种事物，也被别的事物所制胜，就像金木水火土五行相互克制一样；有生有死，万物都是这样；有能有不能，各种生物都是这样；有利有弊，形势总是这样。

　　凡是有形的事物，没有不可被认识的，凡

Qi and *Zheng*

All things between heaven and earth follow these rules: When something has reached its extreme, it starts to develop in the opposite direction; when something has waxed full, it then wanes.... Flourishing and fading succeed each other. This is exemplified by the succession of the four seasons. Something prevails only to be prevailed over. This is exemplified by the way the *wuxing* (五行), or the five elements, (*tr.*: *metal, wood, water, fire and earth*) interact. No living being can escape the cycle of life and death. That is in the nature of life itself. Capability and incapability coexist. That is in the nature of all things. Advantages and disadvantages exist side by side. That is in the nature of all situations.

Therefore, all things and situations with form (*xing* 形) can be named and recognized. All

【原文】

可胜。故圣人以万物之胜胜万物，故其胜不屈。战者，以形相胜者也。形莫不可以胜，而莫知其所以胜之形。形胜之变，与天地相敝而不穷。

形胜，以楚越之竹书之而不足。形者，皆以其胜胜者也。以一形之胜胜万形，不可。所以制形壹也，所以胜不可壹也。

【今译】

是能够认识的事物，没有不能被制服的。所以智慧高超的人运用万物各自的特长制服万物，其制胜的方法是无穷无尽的。作战是运用有形的事物相互制胜的。有形的事物是没有不可制胜的，但是未必知道用什么样的事物制胜它，世上万物相互克制变化，与天地共存而无穷无尽。

有形体的事物相互制胜的事例，就是用尽楚国和越国的竹子，也不能书写完。有形体的事物都以其特长去制胜别一种事物，以一种事物的特长去制胜万物，是不可能的。所以一种事物制胜另一种事物的原理是一样的，要用哪种事物才能制胜哪种事物却不是一样的。

that is named and recognizable can be prevailed over. Thus, the sages know how to use the characteristics of things to overpower them, and there are inexhaustible ways of overpowering things and controlling situations. War is a contest between dispositions seeking to prevail over one another. All distinguishable dispositions can be prevailed over. The question is whether you always know the right method to use to overpower a particular disposition. The changes in the mutual checks among things in the world are as everlasting as heaven and earth and truly inexhaustible.

Examples of this are so numerous that you can exhaust all the bamboo in the states of Chu and Yue and still cannot record them all. (*tr.* : *During the Warring States Period in Sun Bin's days , people used bamboo strips to write on.*)

All things with form use their own special characteristics and advantages to prevail over others. It is impossible, however, for any one thing to use its advantages to prevail over all other things. Therefore, while the principle of one thing prevailing over the other is universal, you still have to find out which thing to use in order to overcome another for each situation is different from another.

【原文】

故善战者,见敌之所长,则知其所短;见敌之所不足,则知其所有余。见胜如见日月。其错胜也,如以水胜火。形以应形,正也;无形而制形,奇也。奇正无穷,分也。分之以奇数,制之以五行,斗之以□□。分定则有形矣,形定则有名〔矣〕。……同不足以相胜也,故以异为奇。是以静为动奇,佚为劳奇,

【今译】

因此,善于用兵打仗的人,看到敌人的长处,就知道它的短处;看到敌人的弱处,就知道它的强处。预见胜利,就像看太阳和月亮那样清楚;克敌制胜,就像用水灭火那样稳操胜券。以常规战对付常规战是正,以变幻莫测战法对付常规战是奇。奇正变化无穷,全在于部署兵力。按照编制序列区分各部队所担负的奇正任务,用五行相克的道理对付敌军。兵力部署既定,就构成了阵形,阵形既定,就会被人识别,〔既被认识,就可能被击破〕,所以每次作战都采用相同的阵法,是不足以取胜的,只有采用不同的战法才能出奇制胜。因此,我以静示敌以动出奇;以逸示敌

Therefore, he who is adept at war can infer from the enemy's advantages his disadvantages. He can also tell where the enemy's strength lies from his weaknesses. He sees the way to victory as clearly as he sees the sun or the moon. He knows how to win as he knows how to quench fire with water. Using regular warfare to combat regular warfare is *zheng*. Using irregular warfare to combat regular warfare is *qi*. There is no end to the interchange between *qi* and *zheng*. It all depends on how you deploy your forces. Assign the different units with *qi* and *zheng* tasks and use the law of mutual checks among the five elements to cope with the enemy.... Once the deployment is decided on, the formation takes shape; and once the formations take shape, they will be recognizable; and once they are recognized.... If you use the same battle formation every time, you will not win victory. Only when you use different formations in different circumstances will you be able to defeat the enemy by a surprise move. Thus, I shall give the enemy an impression of inaction and then take him by surprise; the

341

【原文】

饱为饥奇,治为乱奇,众为寡奇。发而为正,其未发者奇也。奇发而不报,则胜矣。有余奇者,过胜者也。

故一节痛,百节不用,同体也。前败而后不用,同形也。故战势,大阵□断,小阵□解。后不得乘前,前不得然后。进者有道出,退者有道入。

赏未行,罚未用,而民听令者,其令,民之所能行也。赏高罚下,而民不听其令者,其

【今译】

以劳出奇;以饱示敌以饥出奇;以治示敌以乱出奇;以众示敌以寡出奇。被敌发觉的行动是正,未被敌发觉的是奇。出敌不意,击敌措手不及,就能取胜。掌握多种出奇制胜的战法,就能取得更大的胜利。

所以,身上一个关节疼痛,其他关节也不灵活,是因为它们在同一个身躯上。前阵失利,后阵也失去作用,是因为都在同一战阵之内。所以,大阵形〔不可被〕截断,小阵形〔不可被〕冲散。军队后队不得超越前队,前队不得退到后队,前进有路可进,后退有路可退。

赏罚并未施行,而士卒都能听从命令,是因为这个命令是士卒们力所能及的。厚赏重罚,而士卒仍不听从命令,是因为这个命令是

impression of being tired when in fact I am rested; of being starved when in fact well-fed; of confusion in the army when in fact there is order; and of being few in number when in fact my troops are many. Any move that is detected by the enemy is *zheng*, that which is undetected is *qi*. Victory is assured when the enemy is caught unawares and unprepared. Once you have mastered the way of defeating the enemy by surprise moves, you will be able to win great victories.

The reason why all your joints feel out of place when one of them hurts is they are all parts of the same human body. When the front ranks meet with a setback, the rear also suffers, because, as parts of the same battle formation, they are closely linked. That is why the main ranks must not be intercepted and the minor ones must not be overwhelmed and dispersed. The forces in the rear must not supercede the forces in the front, neither must the forces in the front get behind the forces in the rear. Thus, the way is open when the troops advance or retreat.

When your orders are within the capabilities of the troops, they will obey them regardless of reward or punishment. When your orders are beyond their capabilities, they will disobey them

【原文】

令,民之所不能行也。使民虽不利,进死而不旋踵,孟贲之所难也,而责之民,是使水逆流也。故战势,胜者益之,败者代之,劳者息之,饥者食之。故民见□人而未见死,蹈白刃而不旋踵。故行水得其理,漂石折舟;用民得其性,则令行如流。

四百八十七

【今译】

士卒们力不能及的。让士卒在极不利的形势下冒死前进,就是孟贲那样的勇士,也很难做到,却要求一般士卒做到,就好比要河水倒流一样。

所以,作战要因势利导,对胜利之旅要增加兵力,战败的更换部队,疲劳的要进行休整,饥渴的给予饮食。这样,士卒们就会面对敌人舍生忘死,脚踏利刃也不后退。就像水势顺流而下,可以漂起石头,毁折船只;用兵能掌握士卒的心意,军令贯彻就能像流水那样畅行无阻了。

despite handsome rewards or severe punishment.
When you order the troops to risk their lives and
advance under extremely unfavorable conditions,
even brave men like Meng Ben won't be able to
live up to such a demand, not to say ordinary soldiers. That would be like asking the water in the
river to flow upstream. So the thing to do in war
is to guide the soldiers according to their circumstances. Reinforce those who have scored victory; replace those who have suffered defeat; let
the battle-fatigued rest and recuperate; and pro-
vide the hungry with food. The troops will then be
ready to advance fearlessly and they will not turn
back even if they have to walk on sharp blades.
Just as water rushing downstream can move rocks
and overturn boats, so once you have won the
support of the troops, they will advance as ordered with the impact of an avalanche.